WORLD WAR I

1914 – 1918 IN THE TRENCHES

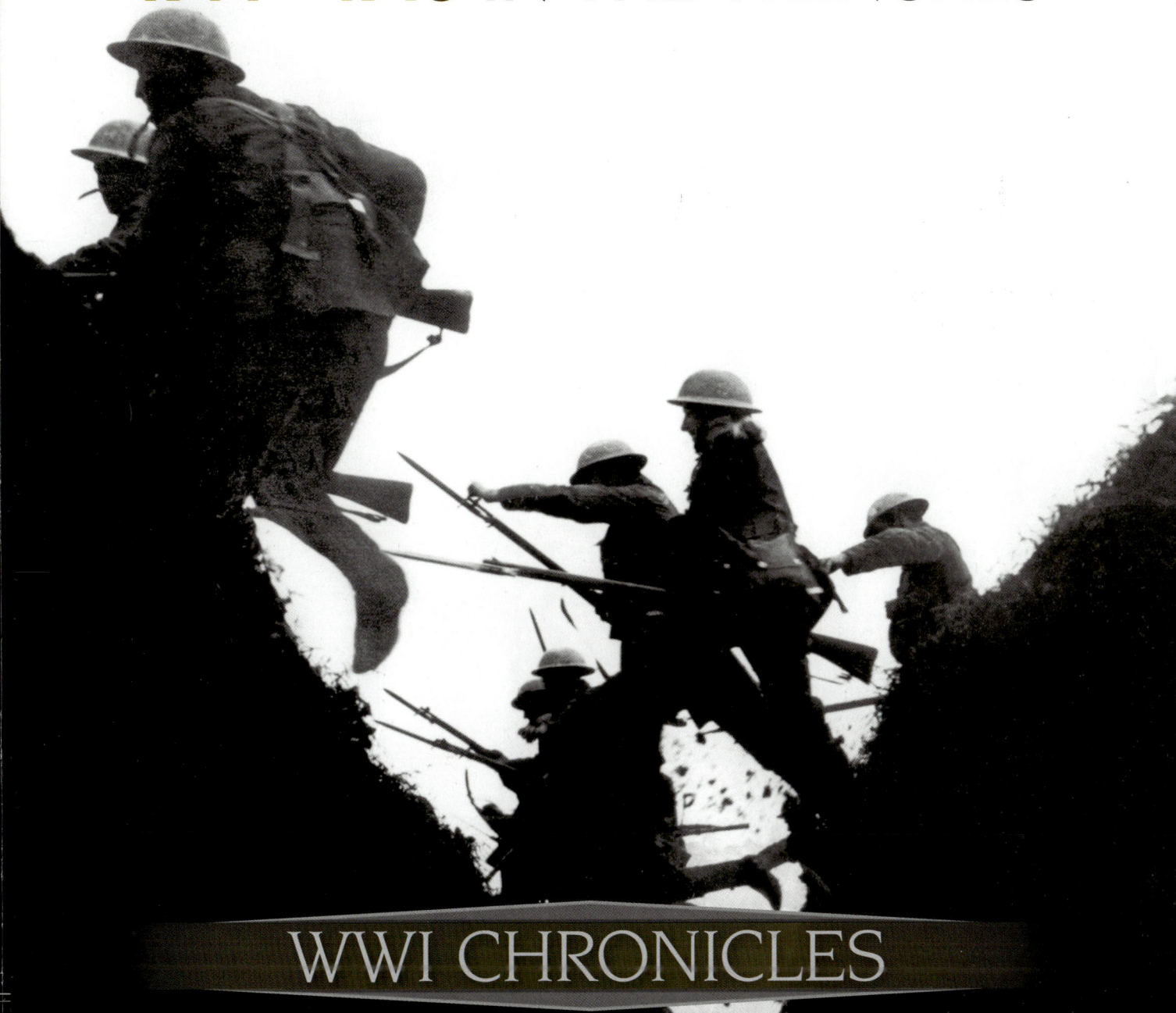

WWI CHRONICLES

Contents

2

3

First published in the UK in 2013

© Instinctive Product Development 2013

This edition published by Park Lane Books

www.parklanebooks.com

Printed in China

ISBN: 978-1-906969-38-7

Designed by: BrainWave

Creative Director: Kevin Gardner

Written by: Adam Powley

Images courtesy of Mary Evans Picture Library, PA Photos, Mirrorpix, and Wiki Commons

www.maryevans.com

Introduction

"*To us in America, the reflections of Armistice Day will be filled with solemn pride in the heroism of those who died in the country's service and with gratitude for the victory, both because of the thing from which it has freed us and because of the opportunity it has given America to show her sympathy with peace and justice in the councils of the nations.*"

– **President Woodrow Wilson**

Each year on the 11th hour, of the 11th day, of the 11th month, people across Britain and other Commonwealth nations gather to pay their respects to the people that took part in one of the most extraordinary events in history. In America, on Veterans Day and Memorial Day, millions more reflect on the sacrifice of generations past. On these somber and moving occasions, people honor the soldiers, sailors, airmen, and civilians who either lost their lives, were injured or imprisoned, made refugees, or in some way took part in one of the largest conflicts mankind has ever engaged in. Other wars resulted in greater casualties, lasted longer, and had an arguably more fundamental effect in their aftermath, but perhaps no conflict resonates so poignantly as World War I.

The Great War, the global war, the "war to end all wars" – a century on from that terrible, colossal conflict, the battles and experiences are fading from memory to become part of recorded history. The last warriors have ended their long and remarkable lives. The sun has finally gone down on those who could recall with heartrending emotion but quiet dignity the horrific reality of what it was like to be there in the trenches, the skies, and at sea. In the famous words of Laurence Binyon's poem *For The Fallen*, written in October 1914 to commemorate the early casualties of the war, "They shall grow not old, as we that are left grow old: Age shall not weary them, nor the years condemn. At the going down of the sun and in the morning, We will remember them."

That so many still remember the war and those who fought in it is testimony to its significance. It was the first truly global war, fought with all the lethal potential that modern industrialized states had at their disposal. The conflict raged across the continents, pulled nation after nation into the fighting, and sowed the seeds for another, even more costly war 20 years later. The map of Europe was redrawn; empires crumbled, new nations were forged. It transformed the ways wars were fought, how societies were led and organized, and provided the spark for revolution.

Remarkable new weaponry made its first appearance, from flamethrowers to the mechanized iron beast of the battlefield, the tank. Guns increased in size, range, and deadly intent, while machine guns wreaked terrible devastation upon near defenseless human flesh. Communications underwent dramatic change and were brought into the modern electric age. Tactics altered, the organization of armies, navies, and emerging air forces reconfigured.

War was pursued both on the ocean waves and beneath them in the shape of mighty battleships and deadly submarines. Aircraft made their first concerted presence felt, waging combat against each other, on troops far below on the ground, and even bringing civilians – who in wars previous had enjoyed relative

■ **ABOVE: The annual Veterans Day parade on Fifth Avenue in New York.**

safety well behind the lines – into the front line.

World War I's origins were complex and varied, but with the benefit of hindsight the epic conflict had an inevitability about it. Powerful and ambitious nations were competing for supremacy and wealth, younger states were growing in influence, and whole peoples under the heel of imperialism or oppressive rule looked to assert their independence and desire for freedom. The resulting tensions propelled the world into the heat of battle and, for four long years, the resulting carnage threw the world into bloody turmoil.

In western Europe, war of attrition and the miseries of the trenches created massed graveyards for millions

■ **ABOVE: A British tank in action in France, 1917.**

■ **BELOW: Tyne Cot Cemetery at Passchendaele, Belgium – the world's largest World War I cemetery of the Commonwealth.**

who had willingly signed up to join the fray or been compelled to do so. In the Middle East, empires clashed head on. Vast and powerful fleets

played a game of cat and mouse punctuated by awesome exchanges of fire on the high seas. A new breed of war hero emerged high in the sky, before the leader of the new world, the United States, hitherto reluctant to join the disputes of the old world, made its decisive entry into the fighting, helping turn the tide of battle against the powers that had fired the first shots.

The eventual triumph of the Allies that was so hard-earned promised much for the victors, but the yearned-for peace and dreams of prosperity did not materialize for so many who took up arms. There was a sense of hope that the armistice did not deliver on and it had lasting and bitter consequences, giving rise to totalitarian regimes, economic suffering, disease, poverty, and the laying out of another path to another war – this time even costlier than the first.

Over 65 million people were mobilized in the pursuit of the war. An estimated 10 million combatants were killed, while many more servicemen and civilians went missing or died of starvation, disease,

and other causes, with many more millions injured, dispossessed, or their health damaged and their lives cut short soon after. The true total figure is still uncertain, illustrating the sheer scale of suffering.

Beautifully maintained war cemeteries and monuments are a moving symbol of the cost of the conflict. World War I never was "the war to end all wars," but it gave many men and women cause to campaign with great passion for peace, and to express their feelings in some of the most moving art of the 20th century. The novels and plays, paintings, and poetry helped to articulate memories and experiences the modern reader, listener, and viewer can barely comprehend – but the vividness of those years still resonates today.

■ **ABOVE:** The British submarine E8, a sister vessel of the E9 that torpedoed the German cruiser *Hela* off Heligoland. (The *Illustrated War News*, September 23, 1914)

Chapter One:
The Coming Conflict
1871 – 1914

■ **ABOVE:** The proclamation of the German Empire in the Hall of Mirrors of the Palace of Versailles. The Iron Duke appears in white. The Grand Duke of Baden stands beside Kaiser Wilhelm, leading the cheers. Crown Prince Friedrich, later Friedrich III, stands on his father's right, January 18, 1871.

All wars have numerous causes and turning points. The connections of history entail a succession of events and themes that build up to history-defining consequences. But if there is a single starting point in the journey to World War I then the unification of Germany in 1871 is a key milestone.

The creation of the militarized German state came in the aftermath of Prussia's victory over France a year before. The architect of that triumph, Prussia's chancellor, "The Iron Duke" Otto von Bismarck, used it to unite German-speaking peoples and define a new and large nation at the heart of the continent. This new state had a massive and growing population of over 60 million, with Kaiser Wilhelm II as its head. Germany now presented a new and potent rival to the existing "Grand Powers" of Europe.

France, which had lost the provinces of Alsace and Lorraine as a result of the conflict, saw Germany as a direct competitor. Britain, for decades the pre-eminent industrialized world power with a vast overseas empire, viewed this new Germanic state as a threat to its rule, influence, and economic interests. France and Britain had been sworn enemies for centuries and, even though there had been peace between the two for decades, it was an uneasy one. Even

of change both at home and abroad. Yet both Austria-Hungary and Russia had eyes on expansion and sought to exploit the decline of the Turkish Ottoman Empire in southeastern Europe, the Russians in particular seeking to support fellow Slavs and Christians in the Balkans and Greece.

France may have dispensed with her monarchy in 1789, but added to the picture were the bewildering connections between the royal dynasties that still ruled much of Europe. When Britain's Queen Victoria died in 1901, the great heads of state attended her funeral, including her son King Edward VII, joined by his cousin Kaiser Wilhelm II, and Tsar Nicholas II who was related to the British Royal family through marriage. Within 13 years these families would be at war with each other.

A prime mover in this march to conflict was Wilhelm II. Aggressive and ambitious, he was determined to increase Germany's power and gain advantage over his nation's rivals. Uneasy alliances and treaties had been agreed between the

■ ABOVE: Otto von Bismarck, Prussian statesman and first chancellor of the German Empire.

■ RIGHT: The royal mourners, crowned heads, and princes and princesses attending the funeral of Queen Victoria in 1901.

so, the prospect of Germany flexing her muscles gave the two nations common cause for concern.

Thrown into this volatile brew were three powers in decline. The Austrian-Hungarian Empire, also known as the Habsburg Empire, dominated great swathes of central Europe and part of the Balkans but was plagued by rebellions from its subjugated peoples, belonging to different cultures and speaking a whole range of languages. It was barely held together by an unwieldy and unpopular ruling elite – an issue also facing Russia. While the Tsars ruled their enormous eastern domains and over 160 million peasants with absolute control, Russia was backward in terms of development and fearful

various powers, with Germany and
Austria-Hungary joined together to
oppose the vulnerable pact between
Britain, France, and Russia. In truth,
they were all competing with each
other. While each state developed
at different rates and to contrasting
extents, the Industrial Revolution,
capitalist economics, political change,
and the hungry craving for conquest
and overseas colonies, particularly
in Africa, fueled the rivalry. Britain
had largely prospered in "splendid
isolation" from the troubles of

mainland Europe but needed her
colonies to feed her own people. Key
to this was maintaining control of the
seas via the all-powerful Royal Navy.
All powerful, that is until Germany
began to upgrade her own navy. In
response, Britain developed a new
range of battleships, the Dreadnought
class of vessels that boasted even
more firepower and range. Germany
in turn responded and so the pace of
the arms race quickened.

Tensions increased. Italy joined
Germany and Austria-Hungary's Dual

Alliance, albeit as a member with
great reservations about impending
conflict. In 1904, Britain and France
established the "Entente Cordiale"
– not quite a formal treaty but an
agreement nonetheless that cemented
shared interests and suspicions.
Russia's defeat in the 1905 war
against Japan further stirred a
combustible mix. Germany's support
for Moroccan independence from
France was opposed by Britain and
increased the antagonism for each
other's people in each nation. In

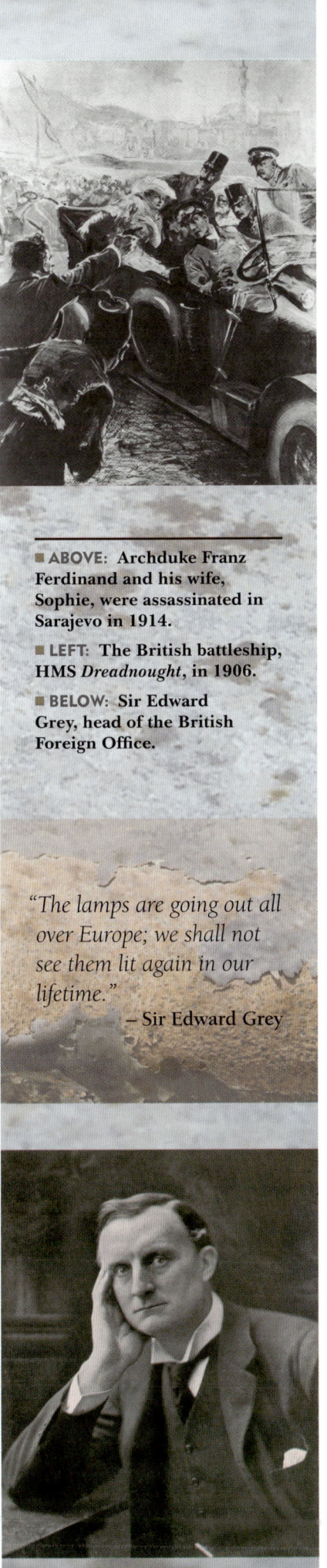

■ **ABOVE: Archduke Franz Ferdinand and his wife, Sophie, were assassinated in Sarajevo in 1914.**
■ **LEFT: The British battleship, HMS *Dreadnought*, in 1906.**
■ **BELOW: Sir Edward Grey, head of the British Foreign Office.**

"The lamps are going out all over Europe; we shall not see them lit again in our lifetime."
– Sir Edward Grey

addition, there were growing political movements in a number of countries, pushing for change and challenging authority. The explosives had been primed; all that was needed was the spark to ignite the inferno.

It came in the troubled Balkan region in 1914. The small states of Serbia and Bosnia-Herzegovina were the scene for increasingly edgy confrontation with the dominant power, Austria-Hungary. Bosnia had been annexed by Austria-Hungary, fearing insurrection and the interest of the Russians. Serbia, once ruled by the Ottomans and determined to remain free, opposed the annexation, which placed many Serbs under the rule of the Habsburgs.

On July 28, 1914, the heir to that throne was on a state visit to the Bosnian capital of Sarajevo. Archduke Franz Ferdinand was traveling with his wife Sophie in an open car through the city, a highly provocative gesture. A bomb had already been thrown at the cavalcade but had failed to harm the Archduke. At around 11am, there was a more decisive act. A teenage Serb nationalist called Gavrilo Princip took aim with a pistol and shot and killed both Ferdinand and his wife.

It was described as the "shot heard around the world" and the echoes soon turned into a deafening roar amid a series of ultimatums and the clatter of troops arming for battle. The Austrians blamed the Serb government for the assassination; Austria was in turn backed by her ally Germany. On July 28, Austria invaded Serbia. In response, Russia began mobilizing for war; Germany demanded an end to the build-up but, with no success, soon declared war on Russia. The domino effect continued apace. Germany sought French neutrality. France declined and, when the Germans falsely claimed France had dropped bombs on German soil, the two enemies drew swords against each other.

The Germans' Schlieffen plan entailed attacking France via neutral Belgium. Britain was determined to defend that neutrality and so, in the face of German refusals to withdraw troops, declared war on Germany on August 4.

The day before, Sir Edward Grey, head of the British Foreign Office, was watching London's street lamps being lit. He commented "the lamps are going out all over Europe; we shall not see them lit again in our lifetime." World War I had begun.

Chapter Two:
"All Over By Christmas"

August 4 **1914** – December 31 **1914**

With war declared, vast crowds thronged the major cities of Europe. From London to Leipzig, thousands took to the streets to acclaim the beginning of hostilities. The sense of expectation, whipped up by patriotic fervor, gave the first moments of the conflict a surreal air. Few had experience of actual warfare and knew nothing of its savage realities. Kaiser Wilhelm's son, the Crown Prince, joked that he would be enjoying "lunch in Paris and dinner in St. Petersburg." The often-repeated refrain was that "it would all be over by Christmas."

Such flippant humor and naivety would be terribly misplaced, and was not the whole picture. Many reacted with a quiet sense of foreboding as they stepped into the unknown. Others, such as Britain's head of the navy, the First Lord of the Admiralty Winston Churchill, had seen war and knew full well what it entailed. Alongside him, Field Marshal Lord Kitchener was appointed secretary for war. To the disbelief of his government colleagues, he said the war would last for three years rather than the three months some anticipated and, dismissive of Britain's existing

reserves, called for a rapid rise in recruitment. He demanded 100,000 – in the event 175,000 volunteered within a week up to September 5, and 750,000 had joined up by the end of the month.

The numbers would prove vital. On August 4, the Germans moved into Belgium. The plan devised by the former chief of staff, Count Alfred von Schlieffen, who died in 1912, proposed a rapid outflanking advance on France via Belgium. Germany needed to move quickly and defeat the French, fearing a fight in the west and the east would prove too demanding. The count's successor, Helmuth von Moltke, put the plan into action.

A visible symbol of German military might made its appearance on August 12, when the huge railway gun dubbed "Big Bertha" opened fire on the fortress town of Liege. This 43-ton artillery piece had to be transported by rail, had a 200-man crew, and took six hours to assemble, but it could propel a 2,200lb shell over nine miles. Within three days, a battered Liege was overcome.

■ **ABOVE: The giant cannon commonly known as Big Bertha, 1914.**

■ **OPPOSITE: Winston Churchill, First Lord of the Admiralty, in consultation with Lord Fisher, First Sea Lord, 1914.**

"My centre is giving way, my right is in retreat; situation excellent. I shall attack."
– message allegedly sent to Marshal Joffre, commander of French forces, by General Ferdinand Foch, during the Battle of the Marne, September 8, 1914

Two days later, French troops entered Lorraine, the disputed province that helped to inspire such a fervent desire for war. The 70,000 men of the British Expeditionary Force (BEF) landed on August 22, under the command of Field Marshal Sir John French, and joined the French in opposing the German advance, thus becoming the Allies in name and substance. At Mons, the invaders were finally halted, but with French divisions in retreat elsewhere, the BEF were at risk of being exposed on their right flank and had to pull back.

The fighting was heavy, costly, and exhausting for both sides, but the sheer weight of German arms began to tell. Paris now lay in the Kaiser's sights. But supply lines were stretched, and the Germans had a nervous eye on the Russians. In East Prussia, the Battle of Tannenberg, August 27-30, was a huge victory over

■ ABOVE: Paris was under threat from the German Army and these French Dragoons were called up to defend the country's capital. The Germans were attacking under the Schlieffen plan, a tactic which involved a lightning attack through Belgium then an advance on to Paris. However, these troops and thousands of others held up the advancing forces and managed to push them back from the capital, September 1914.

the Tsar, inflicting 50,000 casualties and resulting in 90,000 prisoners. But it diverted men and materiel from the west. As a result, the Germans revised the Schlieffen plan and abandoned encirclement of Paris in the west, choosing a frontal assault across the River Marne.

It was a costly error. The French rallied, reinforced by thousands of soldiers dispatched from the capital in fleets of taxis. For two weeks a huge battle raged across a broad front, until the German's themselves were forced to retreat back to the River Aisne. They dug in and were to effectively remain there for four years.

Worn down by stress, von Moltke resigned and was replaced by the minister for war, Erich von Falkenhayn. He sought to gain a new advantage in the "race to the sea" – the desperate fight for control of the coast before winter settled in. A force of Belgians and British were reined against the Germans' four corps. The First Battle of Ypres began on October 15, and was a pivotal contest.

The day before Ypres started, Churchill had arrived in the strategically important port of Antwerp. He announced with great confidence that he would resign his post in government to take command of Allied troops in the area. German artillery, however, ended such plans. Churchill left the city the day before the city surrendered.

As a consequence, Ypres took on profound significance. If the Germans broke through here, the war really could be over by Christmas,

and in the Triple Alliance's favor. Though heavily outnumbered, the experienced BEF soldiers incurred terrible casualties on their largely untried counterparts, the combination of lethal machine gun and Enfield rifle fire halting the Germans in their tracks. By November 11, the German attack came to a weary halt.

Over to the east, the Austrians had suffered badly, their divided forces split between a failed attack on Serbia and opposing four armies of the Tsar in Russian Poland. By the end of the year, the Habsburgs had lost 2 million men, and their plight had forced the Germans to switch divisions away from the Western Front.

Now, the grim reality of the war became apparent. In the west, the stories of atrocities committed against

■ **LEFT:** **British and German troops hold a temporary truce on Christmas Day, 1914. This was the war they had been told would "be over by Christmas." The troops met and exchanged cigarettes and food. The gesture aroused much interest back home but, of course, high command was unimpressed. Soon it was back to the trenches... for another three Christmases.**

■ **BELOW:** **No-man's land seen from the trenches of the 2nd Royal Scots Fusiliers, 7th Division, looking toward La Boutillerie, during the First Battle of Ypres on the Western Front.**

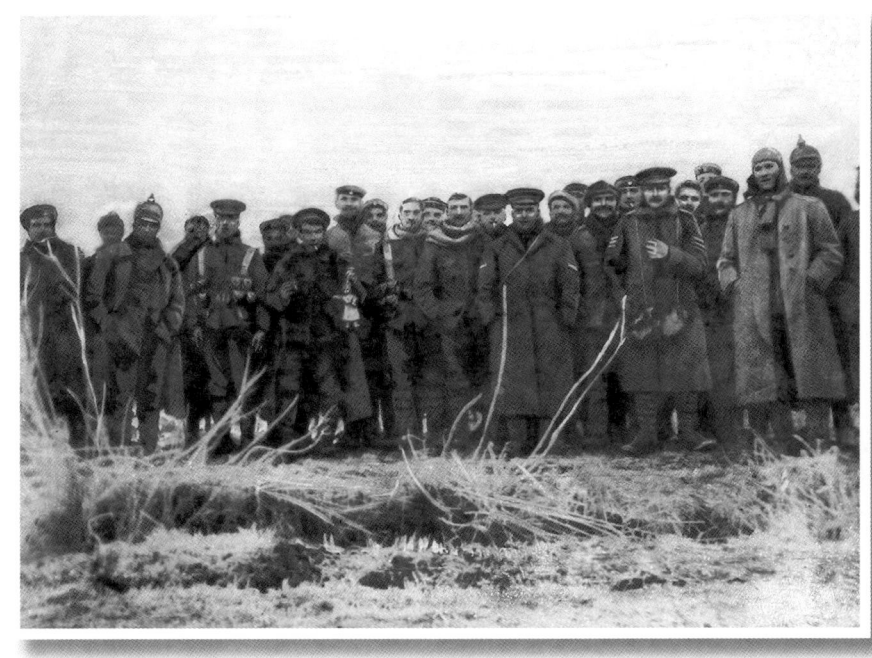

civilians and refugees in Belgium were real enough, but were exaggerated by the Allies for propaganda purposes, and had significant impact on public opinion in America. Canadian troops had answered the call of the mother country and arrived in Britain in October, while Turkey joined the fighting at the end of the month. Their presence did nothing to resolve the situation, however. By December, the front lines had settled down into the entrenched positions that were to define the conflict. The western line extended for nearly 500 miles from the English Channel to the Swiss border, with millions of men facing each other across narrow stretches of no-man's land. It was stalemate.

And then, on Christmas Eve, a remarkable event occurred. German and British soldiers held a brief and strictly unofficial truce. They sang carols, ventured out into no-man's land, and exchanged humble gifts. On December 26 – "Boxing Day" – there was even an impromptu game of soccer.

Commanding officers soon clamped down on such fraternization, however. The business of mass slaughter was to resume soon enough.

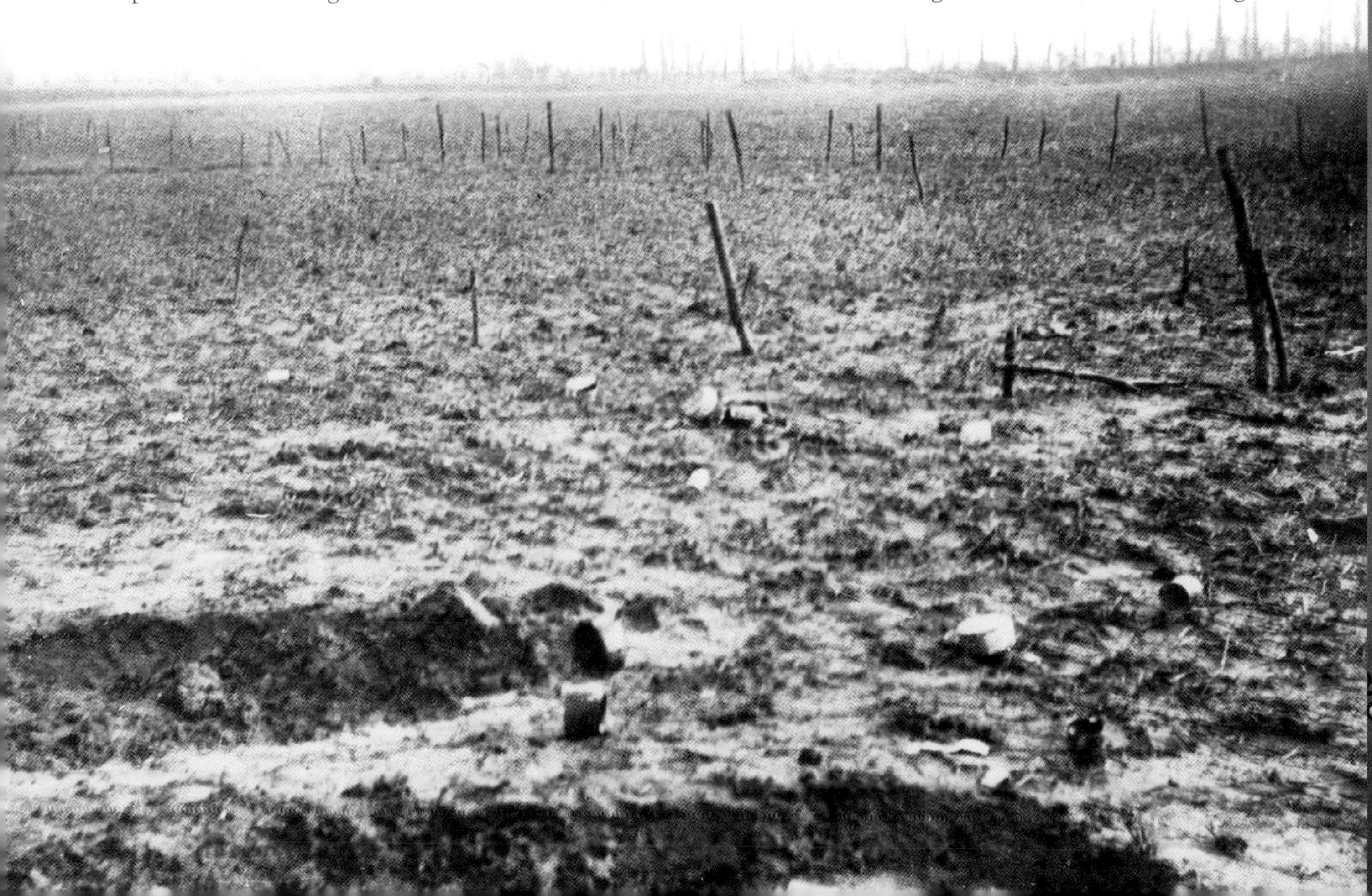

Chapter Three:
Kitchener's Army

"BRITONS Join your country's army!" ran the legend on the recruitment poster. The central image was a picture of the minister of war, Lord Kitchener, the stern-faced, heavily mustached officer wearing a military cap, staring intently, and pointing to an imaginary viewer, with the caption "WANTS YOU." The message was unmistakably clear: it was the patriotic duty of every male Briton of fighting age to answer his nation's call in her hour of need and to join the army. In case anyone was left in any doubt as to what the obligation was, the line at the bottom read "God save the King."

The clamor to respond to Kitchener's call was one of the most remarkable examples of voluntary recruitment ever seen in war. Within a little over a month of the conflict beginning, 750,000 had signed up and the manpower grew further over the next year.

The influx of such huge numbers into uniform reflected the spirit of the times and the almost unique composition of the British Army. The first troops to venture to France, the members of the British Expeditionary Force, were not volunteers but professional soldiers. Unlike in other countries, such as France and Germany, there was no conscription. Instead, the British Army was a comparatively small force of almost 250,000 men, half of them stationed abroad in the various far-flung posts of the Empire.

This army had not fought a concerted battle in Europe since the Crimean War and, while it had been, to an extent, reformed and reorganized in 1907, it still bore

much of the mark of a 19th-century army, particularly in its commissioned officers, drawn largely from the upper classes – it was estimated only 2% had been promoted from the ranks. This was the force that had been damned by the Kaiser as a "contemptible little army," but the proficiency and courage of its soldiers in the early phase of the war rendered Wilhelm's insult as unmerited.

The British could also call on reservists, but the substantial losses of 1914 dictated that the assorted factory workers, clerks, farmers, and tradesmen who had rushed to volunteer were needed on the front line. Many arrived as part of the "Pals Battalions," groups of around 1,000 men joining up from the same town, borough, or workplace. The "Glasgow Tramways Battalion" was made up from employees who worked for the city's transport system; the 17th Middlesex Battalion was comprised

largely of soccer players; the 10th Battalion of the Royal Fusiliers was the "Stockbrokers Battalion;" while the "Accrington Pals" were drawn from the young men of the small Lancashire town. The consequences of having so many men from the same location serving together were to prove tragic.

The influx of nearly 1.2 million men into uniform meant training was limited and geared toward discipline and order. Hierarchy was rigidly enforced. Pay was 35 pence a week for privates, but with food and clothing provided for free; it was a sobering fact that for many of the volunteers, service in the army was an actual improvement on their living standards in civilian life. Recruits often arrived physically weak or undersized – the minimum height for an enlistee was 5ft 2in and even this was reduced later in the war.

Uniform and equipment were

■ **ABOVE:** The 16th Manchesters march past Lord Kitchener at Manchester Town Hall with the rest of the City Battalion, March 1915.

"'Lads, you're wanted!
Over there
Shiver in the morning dew
More poor devils
like yourselves
Waiting to be killed by you."
    – E. A. Mackintosh

■ **ABOVE: Members of the Middlesex Regiment are seen here returning from the trenches in the pouring rain during the Somme campaign. The Battle of the Somme cost the Allies some 420,000 casualties. The Middlesex Regiment had more battalions engaged in this battle and suffered greater casualties than in any other operation on the Western Front during WW1.**

functional, with khaki battledress and puttees – strips of cloth wound round the leg below the knee. The sheer numbers of servicemen in army uniform led to the 1915 Football Association Cup Final, one of the premier events in the British sporting calendar, being dubbed the "Khaki Cup Final," so great were the numbers of soldiers in attendance.

In terms of weaponry, the trusted Lee-Enfield Mark III rifle was a proven and reliable firearm and, in the hands of an accomplished soldier, a lethal and highly effective weapon. Machine guns were to be more murderously efficient. Each battalion had two machine guns – first the Lewis gun and then the water-cooled Vickers that could fire 600 rounds per minute. The Mills bomb provided further and a more explosive means of combat. A cast iron grenade, it was segmented so it would shatter into multiple pieces of shrapnel when it detonated. It was said the Mills bomb was like a bar of chocolate – when it exploded "everyone got a piece."

For all the initial fervor of volunteers, this steady stream of recruits began to dry up by the middle of 1915. The innocent fantasies of young men as to what war was really like had given way to a growing awareness that the Western Front was a killing field. As a result, the British introduced conscription in early 1916. So many officers had been slain that the commanders became younger and younger – many company leaders were barely into their 20s.

summer of 1914 to defend itself.

While the BEF and the French had managed to hold off the Kaiser's advance, the costs had been high, and the new army of volunteers would see modern war for all its horror. It turned civilians into participants in unimaginable slaughter – but millions would not live to tell the tale.

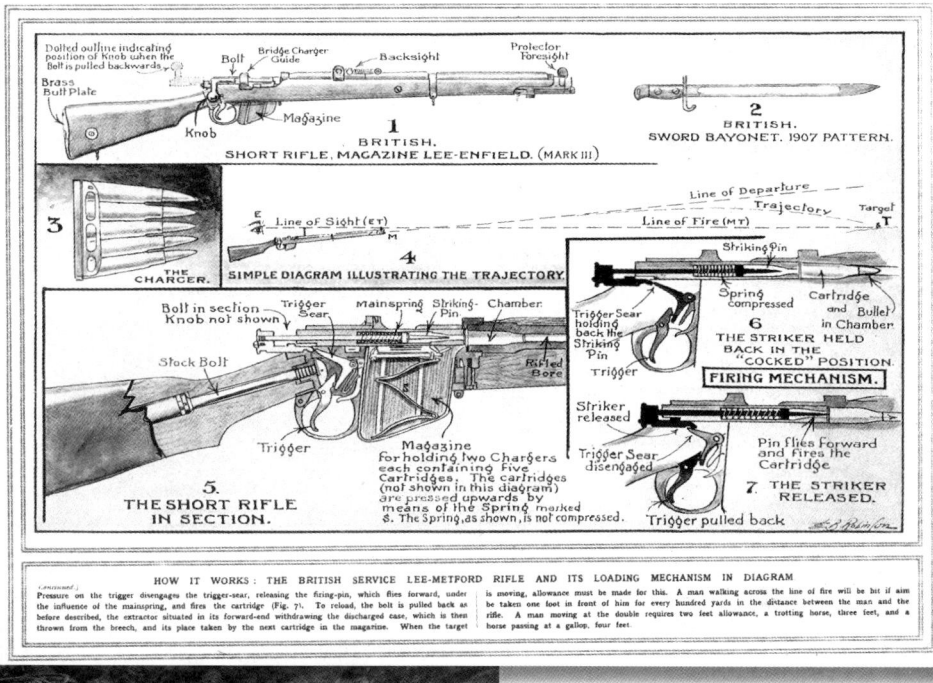

HOW IT WORKS: THE BRITISH SERVICE LEE-METFORD RIFLE AND ITS LOADING MECHANISM IN DIAGRAM

■ **ABOVE:** A multi-part diagram, showing the complex working systems of a short rifle, with a Lee-Enfield Mark III magazine, 1915.

■ **BELOW:** The recruitment of married men – a scene outside Scotland Yard in response to the War Office appeal. At the start of the war recruitment was voluntary, however, by May 25, all able men were conscripted, 1916.

Front-line officers, NCOs, or those from the ranks faced a formidable foe. In truth, the German Army was superior in major respects. It was better armed and trained, and, drawing on a highly militarized and well-established officer class, better led. The French Army was powerful and had more recent experience of continental warfare, but its limitations had been exposed in the war's opening battles. It would require many more than the nearly 3 million who had been mobilized in the

Chapter Four:
The Western Front and Other Battlezones

December 31 **1914** – December **1915**

■ **ABOVE:** German officers in a "splinter-proof" shelter, designed to protect the occupants from shell splinters and shrapnel bullets, 1914.

"… the man had no eyes, no nose, no chin, no mouth – and he was alive!"

– Private L. Mitchell, 24th Field Ambulance, 8th Division

As the clock hands moved round to midnight on December 31, 1914, volleys of fire came over from the German lines. At first, it was assumed it heralded an attack but, with the bullets aimed high, it appeared the fusillade was more a way of ringing in the New Year. Allied troops responded

in kind. Such niceties were not to last long.

After the frantic battles of 1914, the war in the west had settled down into a stalemate. While the Germans might have been outnumbered, they were well organized, and their newly-dug defensive positions gave them the

tactical advantage all along the front. They established well-built lines of not just one, but two, and sometimes three trenches, interlaced with a web of connecting trenches. In addition, they constructed deep dugouts, a factor which was to prove significant later in the war. By positioning

machine guns along commanding lines of fire they had effective control of the battlefield.

The relative outlooks of the combatants had become similarly entrenched. The initial dispute between Austria-Hungary and Russia that sparked the war had been superseded by the more strategic conflict between Germany, and France and Britain. Rivalry for economic and geographical interests was cemented by ideological differences. In Britain, those desperate to defend the Empire, and the more liberal-minded among her political system, found a common enemy in German "jackboot" militarism and the brutal conquest of Belgium. Germans were caricatured as monstrous animals that had to be defeated. In turn, many Germans saw themselves as defenders of cultural and racial purity against the decadent French and the Slavs. France, the senior partner in the Allied effort, with Marshal Joffre as lead officer, was desperate to cast out the invaders who now occupied a fifth of French territory, the people further enflamed with the desire for revenge for 1870.

Having been on the defensive, the Allies now looked to go on the attack. The British had grown in numerical strength, but the volunteer-dominated

■ **ABOVE: Field Marshal Sir John French led the BEF from August 1914. He is seen here (left) with General Joseph Jacques Cesaire Joffre (center), French general, with a party of British and French staff officers, walking through a field, 1915.**

■ **BELOW: A contingent of German prisoners from Neuve Chapelle are seen here passing through Handforth, Lancashire, on their way to the Handforth 3, Queen's Ferry prisoner of war camp, c. March 1915.**

army lacked training, experience, and the required firepower. British artillery was dominated by field guns, which fired shrapnel shells. What was required were heavy guns firing high explosive munitions to damage the German trenches and lay waste the extensive stretches of barbed wire.

The pressure to commit to the attack came too early, before fresh troops had been properly trained and equipped. Communications were also lacking. Together, all these elements rendered the assaults of 1915 largely ineffective and inconclusive.

21

■ **ABOVE:** Troops resting in a mine crater in the mud at Aubers Ridge on the Western Front in France, May 9, 1915.

Offensives in March were repulsed. The Battle of Neuve Chapelle saw the town recaptured, but the casualty rates were grave. Waves of troops were simply mown down by machine-gun fire; the weapon that had been dubbed the "queen of the battlefields" was now referred to as the "grim reaper."

It was a similar story in the Anglo-French offensive at Artois in May. The fighting around Aubers Ridge became a scene of carnage, and men were either on the receiving end or witness to appalling injuries. Seeing the devastation wrought by machine-gun fire and shells sent some men mad. As Private L. Mitchell of the 24th Field Ambulance, 8th Division, recalled in Lyn MacDonald's *1915*, "I never saw any attack with so many men with bullet wounds as at Aubers Ridge… when we took the bandages off we

saw the man had no eyes, no nose, no chin, no mouth – and he was alive!"

Mitchell was ordered to administer an overdose of morphine to put the soldier out of his misery.

Such dreadful scenes were common. At Ypres, the scene of bitter fighting in 1914, the second battle for the town began in April 1915 in an isolated example of the Germans going on the offensive in the west that year. The battle – actually a series of battles around the Flanders town over a period of months extending into September – was notable for a number of elements other than the by-now familiar horrendous casualties: the presence of multi-national forces (Algerians fought for the French, Canadians for the British) and the advent of a new weapon of terror – poison gas (see page 24).

The failure to gain significant

advantage at Ypres and then exploit the partial gains at Loos in September cost Sir John French his job and he was replaced as commander of British forces by General Sir Douglas Haig on November 19, 1915. By then, the war had spread and taken significant turns in other theaters. Two major developments revolved around the activities of two nations in particular. Italy had originally been part of the Triple Alliance with Germany and Austria-Hungary, but was determined not to declare war. The Italians were encouraged to join the Allies by the Treaty of London, signed on April 26, which promised the handover of Italian-speaking regions south of the Alps that had been controlled by Austria-Hungary. Italy then declared war on Austria-Hungary but with punishing consequences for her armed forces in a long and debilitating campaign in the north of the country.

Turkey had been wooed by both sides but the decision of the British to withhold two Dreadnought-class battleships they were building for the Turks enabled Germany to tighten its embrace of a potentially vital strategic ally. In October 1914, Turkey thus entered the war on the side of the Central Powers, and attacked Russia's Black Sea port of Odessa, while German influence and support increased through 1915. The entry of what remained of the Ottoman Empire was to have deadly ramifications for British, French, Australian, and New Zealand troops through spring to the fall at Gallipoli (see page 28).

Fighting began to rage around the globe. Germany's imperial dominions were of more symbolic than strategic importance, but blood was shed in the Pacific and in Africa, drawing in yet more peoples from more nations into the conflict, and further stretching the Allies' resources. In the Balkans, the Serbs were all but liquidated. On the Eastern Front, the situation was critical as Russian forces were pushed back. What it had in sheer numbers, the Russian Army lacked in modern equipment and weaponry and it was routed across the region by the more technologically advanced Germans. The strategic importance of these successes was debatable, but the savagery of the fighting and the inhuman treatment of millions of refuges in Poland, the Baltic States, and elsewhere was all too evident.

■ ABOVE: **General Sir Douglas Haig seen here at an army camp in Northern France, c. 1916.**

■ BELOW: **South African gunners, with their pet zebra, in East Africa, c. 1916.**

Chapter Five:

Ypres and the Horrors of Gas

April **1915** – May **1915**

On April 13, 1915, a German soldier called August Jäger decided to desert, crawled through no-man's land in the Ypres salient, and gave himself up to the French. Desertions were not unheard of but what Jäger was carrying marked him out. He was equipped with a respirator and, under interrogation, readily talked about the Germans having "gas cylinders," and how their poisonous contents would soon be used against the Allies.

Jäger's admission was a signal of a terrible new phenomenon. The war had already sunk to nightmarish depths in terms of its scale and suffering. Now a frightening new weapon was about to make its significant presence felt and further ratchet up the sheer terror of fighting on the Western Front.

Chemical warfare had long been in the minds of military planners and had been briefly used in the east against the Russians, but the attacks by the Germans in the spring of 1915 represented a terrifying escalation in the deployment of poison gas. In the early morning of April 22, Jäger's warning came true. Along a four-mile section of the front line, German troops turned the valves on canisters and a strange visible gas wafted across the battlefield, spread by a gentle northeast breeze.

The first soldiers to be exposed were French and colonial troops from North Africa. They sensed an odd smell at first – a mixture of pineapple and pepper – before the symptoms struck: a burning sensation in the lungs and eyes. On contact with water the gas formed a lethal acid that destroyed soft tissues. The mouths of sufferers frothed and they spat blood, were bent double by terrible sickness and nausea, before many died a slow, agonizing death through asphyxiation.

An estimated 4,000 died or were injured in the first attack, not counting the German soldiers who released the gas only for it to waft back into their faces. This early chemical warfare was an inexact science, but it had a dramatic impact, clearing whole stretches of enemy positions. Exposure prompted an instinctive reaction to run, but this simply presented a machine gunner with an easy target. At Ypres, it was the Canadians who found some means to counter the effect. They urinated into their own handkerchief or patches of cloth and tied these over their mouths and noses, the ammonia in the urine providing a crude method for neutralizing the effect of the acid.

The Canadians fought courageously at the village of St. Julien and played a vital part in restricting the German advance during

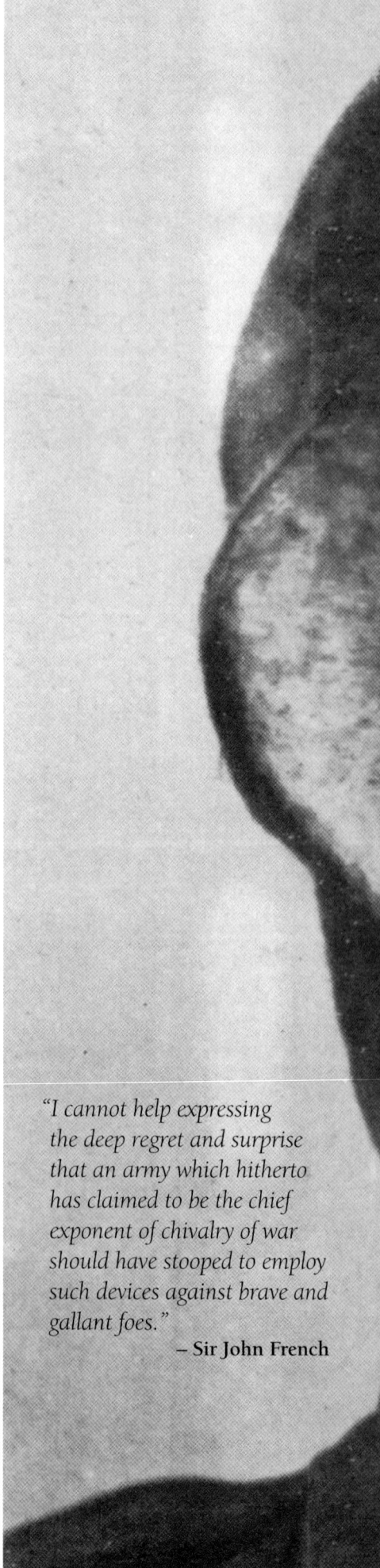

"I cannot help expressing the deep regret and surprise that an army which hitherto has claimed to be the chief exponent of chivalry of war should have stooped to employ such devices against brave and gallant foes."

– Sir John French

■ **RIGHT: A British soldier in the "anti-gas helmet" gas mask in 1915.**

■ **TOP: British troops are seen here transporting ammunition during a gas attack, led by Second Lieutenant E. M. Allfrey in 1917.**

■ **ABOVE: German troops attack the Allied forces with a flamethrower in the trenches, 1917.**

■ **BELOW: Men and their horses took part in army efficiency tests, September 1917.**

the battle. Although the salient was reduced, Ypres itself remained in Allied hands, though at the by-now familiar terrible cost – over 60,000 dead, injured, and missing on the Allied side, with gas taking a heavy toll. The Second Battle of Ypres could even be viewed as primarily an undertaking by the Germans to judge the effectiveness of chemical warfare.

Soon the Allies returned the favor and used gas against the Germans at Loos. Indeed, the desire on both sides to defend against gas attack and reciprocate with improved effectiveness led to a ghastly escalation in poison warfare technology. Phosgene gas wrought even greater damage than chlorine gas, and was so dense that it would cling to the ground and settle in shell craters and trenches. Dicloroethylsulphide, named "mustard gas" for its distinctive odor and color, represented the nadir of the chemical warfare campaign, blinding anyone exposed to its toxic effects and drowning victims in their own blood.

Attempts to protect individuals against gas were rudimentary but became moderately more sophisticated with the advent of flannel or rubberized gas masks and goggles that offered some, but not complete, protection. And the sight of armed men in their masks gave the images of warfare yet another deadly perspective. Artillery shells were adapted to fire gas at significant distances and with greater precision, but the use of such weapons was indiscriminate and their effectiveness debatable. With improvements in rapid reaction to gas attack and enhanced medical treatment, overall casualties during the war as a result of gas were relatively light. The awful suffering and terror they caused was undeniable however, and lasting: many who survived were left in poor health for the rest of their lives.

1915 would also see the presence of other terror weapons. Flamethrowers had long been considered in warfare without particularly successful practical application. The German flammenwerfer, however, lived up to the billing. It was first used against the French at Malancourt in February and then the British at Hooge. The concept was brutally simple: operators would fire a jet of flame 20 to 30 feet long, fueled by a gasoline tank strapped to their back. The effect induced understandable panic among those being attacked and, in the ensuing chaos, those attacked would be vulnerable to more conventional threats of machine gun, rifle, and grenade attack. But these early flamethrowers were unreliable, liable to explode and thus killing their operators, and turned the soldiers carrying them into some of the most despised on the battlefield. They were targeted as a consequence. Few would survive if captured alive.

The Allies responded in kind and devised their own flamethrowers but had some of their own secret weapons up their sleeves. On September 15, British military leaders got their first look at a revolutionary new weapon. The actual display was not exactly convincing but there were signs that the engineers might be on to something. They called their prototype weapon a "landship." The world would come to know it as the tank.

■ **RIGHT: A Klaxon horn was used to warn against gas attacks on French trenches, c. 1916.**

Chapter Six:
Gallipoli
February **1915** – January **1916**

Lack of resolution on the Western Front in 1915 led influential figures in Allied high command and government to cast their eyes to the east and, in particular, Turkey. Winston Churchill, as Britain's First Lord of the Admiralty, joined fellow cabinet minister and future prime minister, David Lloyd George, in advocating a naval assault in the eastern Mediterranean.

Turkey as a world power was in decline after centuries of holding significant sway over much of Europe and the Middle East, but it still presented a formidable partner for the Central Powers. In addition, Turkey threatened Britain's presence in the Middle East and Mesopotamia (modern-day Iraq) and thus the Suez Canal, Britain's vital route to the most precious jewel in her empire, India.

Yet the situation also presented a good opportunity for the Allies. If they could defeat or sideline Turkey they could open up a supply route through the Dardanelles, the narrow strip of water that led on to the capital Constantinople which straddled Europe and the Asian mainland. By gaining command via the Channel, Allied shipping could sail on to the Black Sea to aid the Russians, in retreat on their own front and in desperate need of supplies and aid. The southern flank of Germany and Austria-Hungary would also be threatened. The use of the all-powerful Royal Navy, hitherto under-exploited in the conflict, without the need for land troops, also made the concept a tempting one. "Are there not other alternatives than sending our armies to chew barbed wire in Flanders?" asked Winston Churchill.

In November 1914, Churchill had laid out his scheme and, despite opposition from some within the government and military, the operation was given the go ahead. The planning was not thorough, however, and the mistakes would have disastrous consequences. A naval attack through the Dardanelles began in February 1915 but, after initial success against Turkish forts, the minesweeping operation was severely hampered, both by mines and shelling from Turkish guns fired from the Gallipoli peninsula. The Admiralty and the French then sent in old and outdated battleships rather than risk their more valuable modern vessels, but even the loss of these ships forced a change in the plan. The hope to avoid the use of ground troops was in vain. Preparations were made to land a force of British, French, Australian, and New Zealand (ANZAC) soldiers, commanded by Churchill's old friend, General Sir Ian Hamilton.

The lengthy preparations for the landing were not only incomplete and patchy but enabled the Turkish defenders on the Gallipoli peninsula, led by a German commander, Liman von Sanders, to regroup, rearm, and dig in. Therefore, by the time Allied troops made beach landings on April 25, the enemy was well placed to be able to repel the invasion and, while there were isolated successes, Allied soldiers were pinned down on the beaches and hillsides, and incurred terrible losses.

The Australians and New

Zealanders hit the beach a mile north of their intended target, in a small cove, later to be called ANZAC Cove, surrounded by high cliffs. While they made initial headway, they were

28

■ **ABOVE:** Australian troops prepare to embark for the Dardanelles for the landings at Suvla Bay on August 6, 1915.

■ **BELOW LEFT:** General Sir Ian Hamilton (right), General Braithwaite, his chief of staff, and Captain F. Maitland, are rowed ashore in a warship dinghy, Gallopoli, 1915.

■ **BELOW RIGHT:** A Turkish sniper photographed immediately after capture and while he was being brought in under guard, August 5, 1915.

■ ABOVE: A British soldier pays his respects at the grave of a colleague near Cape Helles, where the Gallipoli landings took place, 1915.

"Those heroes that shed their blood and lost their lives… You are now living in the soil of a friendly country. Therefore rest in peace. There is no difference between the Johnnies and the Mehmets to us where they lie side by side here in this country of ours."
– The words of Kemal Ataturk on the ANZAC Cove memorial

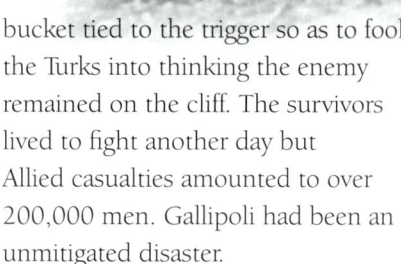

soon faced by determined Turkish opposition, brilliantly led by an officer called Mustafa Kemal. Thereafter, the ANZACS suffered miserably. Trapped in hastily dug trenches on the cliff side, the beachhead a chaotic mess of men and materiel exposed to artillery fire, and waves of men ordered to go on increasingly futile attacks, the campaign became an Australian and New Zealander graveyard. Churchill had hoped to avoid the bloody stalemate of the Western Front. Instead, Gallipoli turned into equally savage and static trench warfare, albeit this time under a merciless Mediterranean summer sun. Conditions were appalling, with diseases such as dysentery rife, rats infesting the trenches, and flies everywhere, their numbers swelled by feasting on putrefying corpses.

At Cape Helles, there was a similar disaster for British troops, and the sea was said to have turned red from the blood of helpless soldiers who never even made the beach. Attempts were made to break the impasse, such as the partially successful landing at Suvla Bay on August 6, but the overall situation was desperate. Trenches were often only a couple of hundred feet apart. The fighting was so ferocious that temporary truces had to be called so that the mounting dead obscuring firing lines could be cleared from no-man's land. Privations on both sides were horrendous and, with the coming of winter, conditions deteriorated even further. The ineffectual Hamilton was sacked and his replacement General Charles Monro soon sized up the situation. "The positions occupied by our troops presented a military situation unique in history," Monro wrote in dispatches, and he demanded a complete withdrawal.

Ironically, this was a great success. Under cover of darkness, the Allies slipped away. They also utilized ingenious methods of deception, such as unmanned rifles fired by the means of water dripping into a bucket tied to the trigger so as to fool the Turks into thinking the enemy remained on the cliff. The survivors lived to fight another day but Allied casualties amounted to over 200,000 men. Gallipoli had been an unmitigated disaster.

Predictably, there were major repercussions. Churchill was in the firing line, and was cast out of major political position. Prime Minister Herbert Asquith's administration was to collapse in part due to Gallipoli, with a new coalition eventually headed by Lloyd George. The impact in Turkey was also profound. While the Ottoman Empire was doomed, the country would be transformed by young army officers. Chief among them was Kemal, who would become known as Kemal Ataturk, the founder of the modern Turkish nation.

Amid this, in 1915, came terrible events in Armenia where the Turks carried out savage retributions. The Christian Armenians, western in outlook and seeking to assert their independence, were held accountable for Turkish military failures and aiding a Russian attack in the north. Assassinations, deportations, torture, starvation, and summary killings led to the death of 1 million Armenians and 1.5 million turned into refugees. The issue of the Armenian genocide remains a bitterly disputed issue in Turkey today.

For Australians and New Zealanders, Gallipoli changed their outlook, too. Britain had been able to call on the support of her colonies and dominions with obedience; indeed Indian troops had been among the first to rally under the Union Jack flag. But further afield the old ties with the mother country had been severely weakened by the defeat at Gallipoli. Many ANZAC troops came to loath British officers for their class-bound imposition of discipline, and their apparent callous indifference and incompetence in the field. This helped forge a stronger national identity in the Antipodes.

Britain's empire was not lost just yet, however. Further to the east, units fought to safeguard oilfields in the Persian Gulf and head off a Turkish attack on Egypt that threatened Suez. The British counterattack led to a new front line in Palestine challenging Turkish interests. Attention was soon to be refocused, however, back in the west.

■ **ABOVE: Australian troops in action at Gallipoli.**

■ **BELOW: Australian engineers build a bridge over the river near the pyramids in Egypt, 1915.**

Chapter Seven:
Tommies in the Trenches

November **1915** – February **1916**

■ **ABOVE:** **British infantrymen occupy a shallow trench in a ruined landscape before an advance during the Battle of the Somme, 1916.**

"A trench is a compromise. It is neither satisfactory as a domicile, nor efficient as a weapon of offence."
– Ian Hay, *The First Hundred Thousand, Being the Unofficial Chronicle of a Unit of Kitchener's Army*

While their comrades suffered on the Gallipoli peninsula, the poor soldiers of the reconfigured BEF tried to live through the miseries of trench life in Flanders and northern France. If any aspect of the four years of fighting came to symbolize World War I it was the grim and miserable daily battle to survive in the field, existing in the most rudimentary of conditions.

Conscription into the British Army had been introduced on February 2, 1916, bringing not just volunteers but young men ordered to join this new kind of war. The gung-ho morale in fervent support of king and country of 1914 had given way to a day-by-

ABOVE: A cartoon by a serving soldier, Sapper E. G. Eschini, showing a British soldier gnawing at the tough and unpalatable biscuits and beef, which were typical rations during World War I.

LEFT: British soldiers go "over the top" in 1916 to attack the German trenches, somewhere in France.

day desire to preserve life – both a man's own and that of his comrades. The bonds of friendship inspired soldiers to look after each other, with the shared experience some way of relieving the suffering. It was not all bad everywhere, but unmitigated misery was common along the 400-mile line.

The trenches themselves were lines of extended holes dug around 7-feet deep. Earth was piled on the front to form a parapet, with more soil at the back to construct a "parados," and steps built up on the inside front face of the trench to form firing positions. Sandbags and timber "revetts"

provided some strengthening of the trench walls. Dugouts were also constructed. These varied in quality but could be as basic as a bare earth hole offering little comfort or protection.

Trenches did not course in straight lines but zigzagged along the front line, with a maze of secondary, support, and communication trenches running behind. They were filled with ranks, NCOs, and junior officers, but the lives they led were far removed from any modern comforts. Men subsisted like animals alongside the rats, lice, and other pests that infested the trench network. Wooden

"duckboards" offered some kind of flooring over the bare earth but, with no protection from the rain, flooding was a constant problem and men were often almost permanently soaked to the skin. Trench foot, a vile infection caused by filthy water, afflicted thousands.

Factoring in the stench from latrines and the nauseous smell of rotting flesh from no-man's land – and even emanating from the walls themselves – and the miseries of trench life were clear. Men had to hunker down below the parapet, else they would risk being shot by snipers. At night there was the fear of attack from raiding parties or being sent on patrol in no-man's land. Even when there was a lull in the fighting there was little respite. Food rations were basic, with "bully" or corned beef and biscuits – washed down

■ **ABOVE: A British firing squad, c. 1916.**

with foul-tasting chlorinated water – an unappetizing staple. Boredom was also a feature. In between the frantic nightmares of battle were long periods of monotonous duties. Gambling, card games, writing letters, singing plaintive or jolly songs, such as *Mademoiselles From Armentieres* (complete with salaciously adapted lyrics), killed time. There was a wit about the names the men gave the towns and locations they fought in. Ypres became "Wipers," while "Sausage Valley" or "Mash Valley" had a gallows humor related to their lethal characteristics. The innate humor of the typical British "Tommy" helped to leaven the gloom. So too did the blessed relief of short spells of leave behind the lines, though many would return to the line nursing monumental hangovers and having caught venereal disease in the large number of brothels that sprang up in the region.

Rum rations helped relieve the tedium, but drunkenness was severely punished. So too were soldiers

deemed to be guilty of cowardice. In such testing conditions it is no wonder many men, some of them little more than teenage boys, cracked and could not face warfare any longer. But the reaction from senior officers was commonly far from enlightened and caring. Shell shock – a nervous breakdown caused by exposure to artillery fire – was a much-misunderstood condition. So too the stresses of combat and seeing so much death and destruction at close quarters. Modern armies recognize

this as post-traumatic stress disorder. The British Army of early 1916, with its rigorously imposed hierarchies and focus on discipline and order, was often merciless in its treatment of brave men who simply could not take it any more. Some "offenders" were condemned to death by firing squad when what they really needed was understanding and care.

The conditions contributed to a growing anger within the ranks, and desertions and even mutinies occurred. Transgressors were subject

to court martial and 351 soldiers serving with the British were executed by their own side, mostly for desertion. The phenomenon of "shot at dawn" remains an enduring stain on the army's reputation.

The vast majority of the troops did not desert, nor mutiny. Most simply strove to survive each day; others displayed astonishing bravery, recklessness, or enthusiasm for combat. But there was a world-weary and fatalistic air among many of the men. The regard of the enemy also changed. Impressionable youngsters, reared on stories of German savagery, found instead that they faced a foe much like themselves. There was an unspoken respect for "Fritz" even if he was one of the dastardly "Huns."

"Fritz" shared many of the discomforts, hardships, and sadness of his adversary, but as was so often the case, his trenches were better designed, built, and maintained, with deep dugouts and bunkers. The Germans were proving nigh on impossible to dislodge with piecemeal attacks. The top brass on both sides realized that the stalemate had to be broken.

"We are standing in water up to our knees. We are supposed to take our puttees, boots, and socks off and smear our feet with this substance... Well, we won't do it."
– Private Edward Roe, East Lancashires

■ **BELOW:** The original caption read British soldiers go "over the top" from a trench in France, 1916. The image was taken by Canadian official photographer Ivor Castle and was widely published as a portrayal of an actual British attack. However, it was actually taken during a training exercise by Canadian troops near St. Pol, France, in October 1916. The breech cover on the rifle of the soldier in the foreground had been edited out and retouched to add the shell burst clouds. After the discovery of the staged image, Castle was recalled to London.

Chapter Eight:
Verdun and the First Day of the Somme

February **1916** – July 1 **1916**

■ **ABOVE: A British Grenadier guardsman keeps watch on no-man's land as his comrades sleep in a captured German trench at Ovillers, near Albert, during the Battle of the Somme, 1916.**

If the ghastly early battles on the Western Front had shocked combatants, an even more horrific fate awaited survivors and new arrivals in the middle phase of the war. Two momentous campaigns in northern France turned the conflict into an escalating slaughter with seemingly little regard for civilized humanity. A century on, the names of Verdun and Somme resonate with the tragic waste of an almost countless number of lives.

There had long been talk among the Allies of a "big push," and by the summer of 1916 – in the absence of Kitchener, who had been killed at sea on June 5 – the order to leave the trenches and go "over the top" sounded along the front.

The strategy behind the Verdun offensive betrayed the thinking of the military top brass. Germany's General Erich von Falkenhayn believed the decisive theater was in the west and devised a massive but pinpointed assault on French lines. The plan was simple: a campaign of brutal attrition to bleed the French dry. "The French Command would be compelled to throw in every man they have," von Falkenhayn claimed after the war. Though it has been contested that these were von Falkenhayn's specific intentions, the outcome was correct.

Verdun's position in the French salient toward the east of the front line posed a threat to the integrity of the German lines and had a historic importance to the French, as a key site of national identity on the natural boundary of the Meuse. It rippled with forts and protective positions and France would indeed fight to the death to protect it.

The offensive began on February 21, 1916, with an enormous artillery bombardment drawing on a stockpile of 2.5 million shells. Despite intelligence warnings, the French were unprepared for the attack and the Germans made initial gains, seizing

"The infantry would only have to walk over to take possession."
– General Sir Henry Rawlinson, General Officer Commanding, British 4th Army

■ **ABOVE: General Erich von Falkenhayn.**

the poorly-defended Fort Douaumont before the French regrouped and launched their own counterattacks.

General Henri-Philippe Pétain – later to earn infamy as the puppet leader of Vichy France during World War II – led the French response. Determined that Verdun would not be relinquished, he ordered repeated attacks to retake any lost ground surrounding it. The Germans were equally unwavering in their commitment to taking Verdun, launching ferocious assaults – including using flamethrowers – on the high ground of the Meuse. The consequence was a battle of sheer carnage, with horrific losses on both sides.

By early June, further German gains were made but, with the launch of the Somme campaign, the Germans' supply of troops on the Verdun front was weakened and the action stalled. This wasn't the end to the fighting, however: the French went on the offensive and regained the territory and the positions they had lost in the preceding months. By the end of 1916, Verdun ground to a halt. Pétain would go on to become French commander-in-chief; von Falkenhayn was eventually replaced by Paul von Hindenburg as chief of general staff.

For those among the poor, long-suffering foot soldiers, gilded promotions or humiliating demotions were the least of their concerns. The longest battle of the war claimed over 350,000 lives on each side, though some estimates cite higher figures. The narrow confines of operations turned the front into a hellish mess of mud and body parts. French soldiers (70% of the army saw action at some point at Verdun) likened it to a "mincing machine." But this was only one example of the dreadful cost of fighting on the Western Front that year.

With the fighting at Verdun hemorrhaging the French Army, her ally

decided to launch another huge attack to the west. The Somme offensive was designed to draw away German forces from the Verdun sector but was also key to Britain's "big push" to try and force a decisive turning point in the war. The French were in support among a multi-national force, but the Somme was a largely British campaign. With the inevitable consequences of the Great War's relentless cull of life, it was the British who therefore bore the brunt of the dreadful toll.

■ **ABOVE: Verdun, ruined by artillery fire in June 1916.**
■ **BELOW: The opening day of the Battle of the Somme. British troops of the 34th Division are seen here during the assault on La Boisselle on July 1, 1916.**

The objective was simple enough. A weeklong artillery bombardment, coupled with enormous mines that had been placed under enemy positions, was designed to churn up German lines, paving the way for massed attack by infantry. With

shells supposed to decimate German troops, destroy their trenches, and cut a swathe through barbed wire, the British mood was confident. Commands were given for troops to proceed across the battlefield in an orderly fashion; some officers expressly prohibited running.

The reality was somewhat different. July 1, the first day of the Somme, was to consign the British Army to its bleakest hours. The familiar initial bombardment had damaged but

failed to dislodge the Germans of the 2nd Army, either well dug in to their network of trenches and bunkers or able to call up reinforcements. Many of the shells failed to explode. As the barrage lifted, the defenders returned to their positions, readied their machine guns, and waited for the infantry to attack. Two minutes prior to this, the vast explosions of the mines provided more in the way of superficial effect than actual impact and served to signal to the Germans that the attack was about to begin. Facing down toward sloping ground, the defenders had ideal lines of fire.

At 7.30am the whistles blew and the men of the BEF – British, Irish, Canadians and other nationalities drawn from across the Empire – went over the top. Huge numbers met either death or injury almost in an instant. Cut down by unforgiving machine gun and rifle fire, and devastating artillery, the troops had pitiful chances of reaching their objectives.

The British Army was, in large part, made up of those "Pals Battalions" that had so enthusiastically gone to war. The idea was to foster a sense of comradeship and local pride. But on the Somme it meant that whole communities had a generation of men cut down in their prime. The Accrington Pals lost 585 men alone.

From Glasgow to Middlesex, Lancashire to Yorkshire, Ulster to Newfoundland, and in many places in between and further afield, families and communities would come to mourn the loss of so many loved ones. The slaughter was almost incomprehensible: by day's end there were over 57,000 British casualties, with nearly 20,000 killed.

The first day was not a complete failure. In the southern British sector, gains were made and, further south, the French captured significant ground thanks to well-conducted attacks and the relatively weaker condition of German defenses. Mistaken in the belief that casualties amounted to 40,000, Haig did not consider the losses "severe."

But, as night fell, and with injured men still suffering agonizing deaths in no-man's land while colleagues made valiant attempts to rescue them, the survivors were left to reflect on the darkest day in British military history. And it was only the first day of a bloody battle that would last four, horrendous months.

■ **BELOW: General Sir Douglas Haig, commander-in-chief of the British Army.**

Chapter Nine:
Tank!

July 2 **1916** – December **1916**

British senior commanders were nothing if not convinced of their own judgment. Despite the decimation of their forces on that terrible first day of the Somme, they regarded their tactics

■ **ABOVE: Canadian troops on a tank.**

as justified, and would continue to send young men needlessly to their deaths in largely futile attacks.

There were disputes between Haig and his 4th Army commanding officer at the Somme, General Rawlinson, but with neither the will nor the imagination to change course, the policy of attrition continued. Planning may have been meticulous but the reality of how attacks floundered in the face of machine-gun fire exposed the fundamental weakness of British tactics. About seven miles of ground had been gained by the campaign's end but at the cost of 150,000 lives out of a total of 600,000 Allied casualties. The hellish sight of already interred bodies being brought to the surface by artillery fire was a sickening indication that this was land that had already been fought over.

It was out of the Battle of the Somme that emerged the popular belief that the ordinary soldiers were "lions led by donkeys." It could be argued that the strategists were adhering to the conventional military wisdom of the time. But here was a callous disregard for the value of human life. Thousands would die in single engagements. The Welsh 38th Division was all but destroyed in attacking Mametz Wood. It took five attacks to capture Pozieres, with the Australians taking 28,000 casualties in a little over six weeks. The Ulster Division's fight for Thiepval was a success but again won at great cost and came over two months after the town was supposed to have been taken.

The slog between Flers and Courcelette followed a similar pattern with little ground gained for dispiriting losses. But there was one feature that marked the operation out. The British had been developing the tank since 1914 – the name came from "water tank," a term coined to aid secrecy. Initial plans for glorified "armed tractors," envisaged by Colonel Ernest Swinton, were rejected but, undaunted, he gained the support of Colonel Maurice Hankey and then the still influential Winston Churchill. The "Little Willie" prototype was followed by "Mother" in early 1916. By the summer, Haig was keen to deploy a serviceable vehicle and the Mark I made its dramatic appearance.

Its 28 tons lumbering along at 4mph, carried a crew of eight in stifling conditions, nearly suffocated by fumes and heat and thrown around like ball bearings. But in its two forms – a "male" version with its two six-pounder guns and three light machine guns, or a "female" model with two heavy machine guns – it represented a fundamental change in mechanized warfare. Of the 49 tanks Haig planned to commit to the battle, only 32 made it to their start lines on September 15. Their presence was piecemeal, the machines spread too thinly across too wide a front, rather than concentrated for maximum effectiveness. They were slow, broke down, were hugely difficult to drive and operate, and could not traverse a number of obstacles. Communication inside and out was virtually impossible. The knowledge of how best to utilize tanks was, understandably, in its infancy. But 12 Mark Is did reach the German lines – six into the village of Flers itself. And they did have a telling impact.

Their performance that day was mixed. In one appalling incident they mistakenly killed a number of British troops ready to go over the top from an assembly trench. Elsewhere, they had an eye-catching effect on the enemy. Lyn Macdonald's book *Somme* features a number of extraordinary first-hand accounts of the tank's combat debut, showing how the Mark Is caused panic among the German defenders.

These tanks were not decisive but they aided perhaps the best success of the campaign, with twice as much ground captured during the attack than on July 1, but for half the casualties. The Germans held the line, though they took a severe beating in the process.

During these latter stages of the battle, "creeping" artillery barrages improved and the coordination between the lifting of shellfire and the advance of infantry was organized more effectively. Some lessons *were* learned and tactics had improved. The Somme did do significant damage to the Germans, who lost up to 680,000 men, and the battle was a signal that the Central Alliance could not win the war of attrition in the west, a factor that proved crucial to the future conduct of the fighting.

But, by mid-November, with the bad weather settling in and turning the already battered landscape into a mud-churned alien world, the offensive was called off. The tank had announced a new development in war, but the long lists of the fallen and increasing numbers of dead with no known grave were the real legacy of the Somme.

■ **BELOW: A Mark I tank in action on the Western Front in 1916.**

Chapter Ten:
Death in the Skies

Prior to the bombardment of the Germans' superbly constructed trench network in the chalky uplands of the Somme, both German and Allied soldiers would have seen a by now familiar sight of the World War I battlefield. Buzzing above them in the skies were aircraft of the Royal Flying Corps, carrying observers to reconnoiter the ground that so many soldiers would lose their lives fighting for.

Airplanes had made a tentative appearance in 1914, aiding cavalry regiments in observation duties. The irony of using such new technology to support a relic of warfare of the past was not lost on the pilots, for theirs was the coming theater of war that would be so decisive in future conflicts.

From the outset of airplane

■ **ABOVE:** **Soldiers inspect the wreckage of Zeppelin L31, which was shot down over Potters Bar by Second Lieutenant Wulstan Tempest, October 1, 1916.**

"Everything depends on whether we have for opponents those French tricksters or those daring rascals, the English. I prefer the English. Frequently their daring can only be described as stupidity."
– Manfred von Richthofen

development at the turn of the century, fears were raised of terror being unleashed from the skies, with no place safe from attack. There were sporadic raids by huge Zeppelin dirigibles dropping bombs on London, the Midlands, and ports.

Zeppelins flew high (up to nearly 14,000 feet) and could carry a considerable bomb load of 4,400lbs. Their attacks spread fear and wreaked havoc: 28 people were killed in the first raid on London alone. But their sheer size made them impracticable. When a Zeppelin was set on fire over London on October 1, 1916, it was reported that the whole of the capital rang with cheers as the flaming airship drifted north, to finally crash in the suburbs.

Zeppelins were also used on the Western Front, but it was the airplane

THE GRAPHIC

AN ILLUSTRATED WEEKLY NEWSPAPER
The entire contents of this paper, both Illustrations and Letterpress, are copyright.

No. 2355. Vol. XCI.
Registered as a Newspaper.

SATURDAY, JANUARY 16, 1915

[PRICE SIXPENCE
By Post, 6½d.

Drawing copyrighted in the United States and Canada.

THE THREAT OF THE ZEPPELIN: GAS-BAG OR TERROR—WHICH?

The much advertised Zeppelins were to have begun their raids on England this week, but so far the atmospheric conditions have been adverse. You will note that the cartoonist, Mr. David Wilson, queries the possibility in the shape of a smoke-outlined point of interrogation.

■ **ABOVE: A cartoon showing the Kaiser's head on the front of a Zeppelin airship, during World War I. The German Zeppelins' first successful raid was on the night of January 19-20, 1915, in which two Zeppelins, L3 and L4, were directed toward the Humber in England but, diverted by strong winds, dropped 24 high explosive bombs and ineffective incendiaries on Great Yarmouth, Sheringham, King's Lynn, and the surrounding villages. In all, four people were killed and 16 were injured.**

that was to rule these particular skies. The initial use was for reconnaissance purposes, gathering vital information on troop movements, concentrations, armaments, and the position of gun batteries. Observations were at first made using the naked eyes of the two crewmen that usually flew in such missions, but the development of more sophisticated photographic technology enabled highly accurate visual reports. Airplanes proved their worth at the battles of Mons and the Marne, supplying crucial information to the Allied infantry on German movements.

France's Aeronautique Militaire initially led the way, but each armed force soon recognized the importance of improving and manufacturing ever-greater numbers of aircraft. Gaining advantage in flight-borne reconnaissance could only be done with command of the air, so there was an inevitable escalation in the air war. Planes had to be made faster in order to escape anti-aircraft fire from the ground, and attacks from enemy aircraft. Fighter planes were rapidly developed to see off this threat to enable observers to carry out their missions. The struggle for advantage fed a cycle of aircraft development, so that by 1916 Allied planes flying over the Somme had the skies virtually to themselves, thus providing highly detailed maps that enabled British gunners to hit German targets with greater accuracy.

The British air force had its roots in an Air Battalion of the Royal Engineers, founded alongside the Royal Naval Air Service attached to the navy. By 1912, the Royal Flying Corps (RFC) was founded. When war began, balloon sections attached to army units provided the mainstay of reconnaissance activity, but the poor observers who manned these static balloons were sitting targets, and soon gave way to pilots flying the new planes coming into service.

De Havilland, Bristol, Avro, and Sopwith were just some of the names of early manufacturers' planes, initially crewed by a pilot and an observer.

Formed into squadrons of 12 planes, the aircrew of the RFC soon earned a distinctive reputation. The need for men who actually knew how to fly an airplane dictated that many of the early pilots were well-to-do gentlemen who could afford to have learned to fly and even own their own airplane in the pre-war era. Flying from and returning to their airfields behind the front line, they enjoyed greater creature comforts than those wallowing in the mud of the trenches. As a consequence, resentments often built up between soldiers and airmen.

The bravery of pilots was undeniable, however. They flew in relatively flimsy aircraft exposed to the elements, hurtling at speed in confused engagements and under fire both in the air and from the ground. British pilots were not initially equipped with parachutes and, with gasoline tanks barely protected from bullets, they were in danger of death or terrible burns. Life expectancy during active service was measured in weeks, rather than years. In 1916, an average of two crew were lost each day; the next year the RFC was losing nearly 50 planes a week.

No arm of the conflict evolved quite so quickly as the air war. Rapid technical improvements meant planes flew higher and faster and were more maneuverable. An airplane arms race gathered momentum with each side gaining the upper hand. Lewis machine guns were mounted on British planes, before the Germans stole a march, with the Fokker Interrupter, which enabled ammunition to be fired directly through the gaps in the propeller blades. Low-level flying tactics were perfected so that planes strafed enemy lines to telling effect, while "dogfights" increased in frequency.

Flying in squadron formation pilots would break off to fight desperate individual battles, offering a throwback to a more chivalrous ideal of one-on-one duels rather than the indiscriminate mass slaughter on the ground. Air aces soon gained a glamorous and dashing character. Albert Ball, Edward Rickenbacker, and George Guynemer all earned fame and renown, but none as widely as Manfred von Richthofen, the acclaimed "Red Baron."

As leader of the "Flying Circus," a crack unit of Germany's top fighter aces, this former cavalry officer flew a distinctive red Albatros D-III and was responsible for an astonishing 80 "kills" in less than two years, until he was shot down and buried with full military honors by his foes.

The supposed romance of the fighter aces belied the true nature of air power, however. Bombing strategy also developed at pace. The Royal Naval Air Service had bombed targets by night as early as December 1914. In the summer of 1917, daylight bombing raids by German Gotha bombers were launched. The policy of strategic bombing was becoming more convincing as the conflict progressed, and its adoption changed the face of warfare as a whole.

■ **ABOVE:** RAF pilots report the position of enemy troops on the Western Front.
■ **OPPOSITE:** A picture of a dogfight during the Great War, September 1914.
■ **BELOW:** Manfred von Richthofen, the acclaimed "Red Baron," sits in the cockpit of his Albatros fighter for a photograph with his squadron, 1917.

Chapter Eleven:
War in the East
1916 – 1917

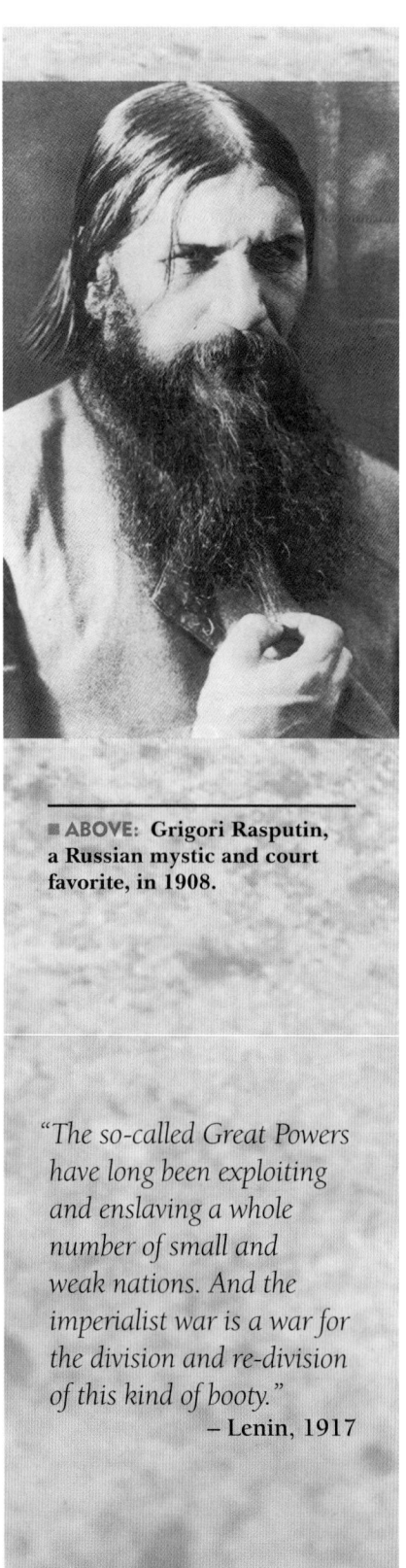

■ **ABOVE: Grigori Rasputin, a Russian mystic and court favorite, in 1908.**

"The so-called Great Powers have long been exploiting and enslaving a whole number of small and weak nations. And the imperialist war is a war for the division and re-division of this kind of booty."
— Lenin, 1917

While the air aces were being celebrated for their headline-grabbing exploits, a rather different war was being fought in the east. The Russians and the Central Powers had waged a war not so much of attrition as a battle of extermination, and it would culminate in revolution.

Russia had relied on sheer numbers from its vast, largely peasant population to feed its war effort but, by 1917, even this resource was being exhausted. Nonetheless, the army that had been "drowning in its own blood," according to one general, was still able to take the fight to the enemy.

The March 1916 offensive at Vilna, led by General Alexei Brusilov, incurred casualties of 100,000. Committed to supporting French and British efforts in the west, Brusilov launched another attack in June on the Galician Front. This time his forces drove a 20-mile gap 60 miles deep, and took 500,000 Austrians prisoner. It was an impressive feat; the Russian Army had improved, and it was now better led, trained, and supplied. Its tactics of concerted and directed force reflected the changing modes of warfare that would break the more general stalemate.

The embattled Russian foot soldier once again fought with typical bravery and tenacity in these battles, but Brusilov and his millions of men could not press home their immediate advantage and they suffered demoralizing reverses as the Austrians fought back. The Tsar's Army were handed the by now familiar crippling losses – almost a million

in total. Their earlier successes had encouraged the Rumanians to join the war on the Allied side, but their entry came too late and their contribution was certainly too little. The Rumanian Army, such as it existed, was trounced as Austria invaded and in the process seized valuable oilfield and grain supplies that the Central Powers craved.

These setbacks had a dramatic impact in Russia itself. The country had already labored under a fraught political situation. Tsar Nicholas had taken charge of the military in an attempt to stiffen resolve and reinvigorate the military, leaving his German wife Alexandra and a coterie of either inept or corrupt politicians in charge of domestic affairs. The political situation was a mess, compounded by the presence of Grigori Rasputin, the monk who held Alexandra under some kind of spell. Rasputin's assassination in 1916 ended the life of one of the more bizarre characters to be privy to world-shaping events, but it did little to remedy the ills of the Russian state.

The economy was in tatters, and there were mutinies in an army now manned by disaffected conscripts whose peasant families back home were facing starvation. In the cities, strikes and street protests sprang up. Brusilov had been made commander of Russian forces in February 1917, but the Tsar's rule was collapsing. Under intense pressure, he was ousted in March, though the hope of the people that the war would then swiftly end was in vain. Under pressure from Britain and France,

Russia and her new reformist government stayed in the fight.

The decision further enflamed the situation. Sensing that a destabilized Russia worked to their advantage, the Central Powers were happy to let Lenin out of exile from Switzerland and travel via Germany, confident that any new Russian government would call off war, thus freeing Germany and Austria-Hungary to focus on the battle in the west.

Lenin's arrival in Russia gave further momentum to the revolutionary fervor. His rallying slogan of "Peace, bread and land" struck a chord with a people sick of war. Lenin and the Bolsheviks took power in October, with enormous consequences for the post-war world. The immediate result was that a peace accord was struck and Russia was effectively out of the war.

The western Allies had now lost a major partner. The war in the east was not all going against them, however. In the Middle East, the British continued to make strides against the Ottoman Empire. Under the leadership of General Sir Edmund Allenby, victory at the Battle of Gaza in January 1917 was a milestone on the road to overall triumph, and by the end of the year the British had taken Jerusalem. Major setbacks in Mesopotamia had dogged the campaign but through 1917 Britain and her colonial troops finally began to prevail.

These efforts were aided by the Arab Revolt, which was in turn invigorated by the extraordinary T. E. Lawrence, an intelligence officer stationed in Cairo. In the vernacular of the time, Lawrence, who had traveled extensively in Arabia before the war, had "gone native."

Almost worshipped by his Arabian followers, he led guerrilla attacks on vital Turkish supply lines and became a near-mythical hero.

With Greece having joined the Allies in mid 1917, the situation at the end of the year had become more clearly resolved. World War I was now a more defined fight in the theater of Europe, involving its major powers and their continental Allies. But by then another partner was poised to join the fight against the Central Powers. As early as April 1917, America had declared war on Germany. World War I was nearing its end game.

■ BELOW: **Lieutenant Colonel Thomas Edward (T. E.) Lawrence, an officer in the British Army, known for his role in the Arab Revolt against Ottoman Turkish rule of 1916-18 during World War I. He was commonly known by his nickname, Lawrence of Arabia.**

Chapter Twelve:
War at Sea
1914 – 1917

Given that the war arose in part due to the build-up of navies and the race to either gain or maintain mastery of the waves, the war at sea had played a relatively secondary role to the major land battles. Yet, in the closing phases of the conflict, one aspect of the naval war would be fundamental to a pivotal event.

The two main protagonists in the war at sea were the British Royal Navy and the German Imperial Navy or Kaiserliche Marine. The head of the latter, Admiral Alfred von Tirpitz, had been determined to match the Royal Navy modern ship for modern ship but, by 1914, Britain still held a numerical advantage. Both sides placed great store by the strategic importance of naval power. Indeed, they viewed it as the most important factor. If one side could destroy the other's fleet it would enable the victor to starve the other into submission. As Winston Churchill said of his naval commander-in-chief, Admiral John Jellicoe, he was "the only man on either side who could lose the war in an afternoon."

The consequence was thus a comparatively limited deployment of naval arms. Ships were initially used for troop movements, supplies to Allies, and shows of strength. The fighting for real began in August 1914 with a number of engagements. First at Heligoland Bight, the Royal Navy sank four German cruisers. Germany suffered another setback when Japan tentatively entered the war on the side of the Allies and took over the German base of Tsingtao in China. The response came with the sinking of three British cruisers and the loss of 1,500 lives in the Channel from submarine torpedoes in September, and there were costly but inconclusive tit-for-tat exchanges in the South Atlantic, first off the coast of Chile and then near the Falkland Islands in December 1914.

Thanks to the possession of German code books, the Royal Navy was able to intercept and see off a German squadron in the North Sea and sink the *Blucher* at Dogger Bank in January 1915, while the knowledge of Kaiserliche Marine intentions

helped to limit the damage and casualties caused by German raids on English east coast ports. But the expected major showdown had not materialized, with the bulk of each fleet remaining safely in harbor.

It was the Kaiserliche Marine High Seas Fleet's new commander, Admiral Reinhard Scheer, who blinked first. On May 31, 1916, the Germans cast off out into the North Sea to take on the Royal Navy's Grand Fleet. The two armadas finally faced each other off the coast of Denmark, in what became known as the Battle of Jutland (or Skagerrak to the Germans). Admiral Franz von Hipper led a feint to draw Admiral Sir David Beatty's force into pursuit to where the bulk of the German fleet would be waiting. Unbeknown to the German commander, the Royal Navy knew of the plan and had itself dispatched Jellicoe's Grand Fleet to spring its own surprise.

The resulting action saw the huge guns of each fleet fire in concerted anger against each other in the only major sea battle of the war. Initial German successes gave way to a fear that they would be annihilated when Jellicoe's force appeared on the western horizon. Scheer turned for home port and Jellicoe, fearing another trap in the form of a submarine attack, did not mount a full-scale pursuit.

The Royal Navy came off worse in

■ **BELOW: The ships that fought off Heligoland, August 28, 1914. This picture shows the first and second squadrons, headed by the *Lion*, *Queen Mary*, *Princess Royal New Zealand*, *Shannon*, *Cochrane*, *Natal*, and *Achilles*. Three German cruisers were sunk during the action in which Admiral David Beatty distinguished himself.**

terms of losses, with the thin armor plating of three battle cruisers leaving them vulnerable to accurate German shellfire. Overall, the Royal Navy lost 14 ships to the Germans' 11, and the loss of 6,000 sailors lives to the 2,500 of the Kaiserliche Marine. The result was a tactical victory for Germany but a strategic defeat. The Royal Navy still ruled the waves, despite the claims of the Kaiser, and the Kaiserliche Marine never risked open battle again.

Both sides sought instead to blockade the other, and this was to have pivotal ramifications. Hemmed in by its opponents, and with its civilian population starting to suffer from malnutrition and disease, Germany sought to exploit Britain's reliance on imports by using its "Untersee" or "U-boats" to wage submarine attacks on merchant shipping. The strategy was stepped up in 1915 with the warning that any vessel entering British waters was in a "war zone," a response to the Royal Navy enforcing a similar policy in the North Sea.

Matters came to a head when the cruise liner, the *Lusitania*, was torpedoed off the coast of Ireland on May 6. Over 1,000 civilian passengers died, among them, crucially, 128 Americans. This led to outrage in America, which had hitherto been

neutral, although largely sympathetic to the Allied cause. As U-boats ramped up their aggression (sinking non-military ships on sight rather than giving warnings and allowing passengers and crew to escape on lifeboats), American anger increased.

Amid conflicting views within government, Germany now considered a calculated gamble. Continuing the strategy would risk America joining the war on the side of the Allies. But even if she did, the damage the U-boats could do to Britain's ability to supply its war effort and feed its people could bring Britain to its knees.

President Woodrow Wilson entered center stage. He had attempted to broker peace deals between the belligerents but the complex negotiations and the fact that both sides felt they could still win the war undermined that hope. Now, the pace of developments quickened. Germany announced it would target *all* vessels from February 1, 1917, leading to Wilson

breaking off relations with Germany. When a cable from Foreign Minister Arthur Zimmermann sent to Mexico proposing an alliance against the US was intercepted, the die was cast. On April 5, 1917, America declared war on Germany.

■ ABOVE: The more fortunate passengers left the torpedoed *Lusitania* as it listed before going down, but 1,198 lives were lost.

"*What happened? The English were beaten. You have started a new chapter in world history.*"
    – Kaiser Wilhelm II, addressing the German High Seas Fleet at Wilhelmshaven, June 1916

Chapter Thirteen:
The Deadlock Loosened

Western Front **1917**

■ **ABOVE: During the spring of 1917 the German forces on the Western Front voluntarily retired from the positions in the Somme at Serre, which they had defended with such stubborness in 1916, to the famous Hindenburg Line – an intricate system of heavily fortified trenches between the Vimy Ridge on the north and the Chemin des Dames ridge in the south. In the background of the photograph there is a sign saying "Old Hun line."**

"There was not a sign of life of any sort. Not a tree, save for a few dead stumps which looked strange in the moonlight. Not a bird, not even a rat or a blade of grass. Nature was as dead as those Canadians whose bodies remained where they had fallen the previous autumn. Death was written large everywhere."

– Private R. A. Colwell

Before American soldiers would be committed to a largely European war, the Europeans would continue to slaughter each other with seeming enthusiasm. The means and tactics would be varied, however.

General Erich Ludendorff, effectively Germany's leader, had expressed his faith that the submarine strategy would eventually prevail. In the meantime, he ordered his land forces to go on the defensive, in part to avoid the kind of loss of life the German Army had experienced during the Battle of the Somme. To facilitate this he ordered the construction of a new defensive line 25 miles to the rear but, this time, instead of a continuous trench line, it was a series of heavily fortified positions with command of the field through concrete pillboxes, artillery, and machine guns. The infantry would be held in relative safety in the rear.

This new position would be dubbed the "Hindenburg Line" (also the "Siegfried Line"), and during their tactical retreat, the Germans applied a scorched earth policy to the French soil they left behind. Almost overnight, the Allies had in their hands the fields they fought so desperately and fruitlessly to gain in 1916, but they inherited a wasteland.

To counter the new German tactics, the French, under their new commander, Robert Nivelle, proposed the development of offensive tactics that had shown promise at Verdun – concentrated and accurate assaults on specific targets followed by equally concerted infantry attacks to open and expand any position that was gained. The British favored a more cautious approach, relying more on artillery to gain limited objectives that would be defended from counterattack while the sights of the guns were recalibrated to the next target – a tactic called "bite and hold."

The two concepts were soon put into practice. Nivelle's plan floundered in the disastrous attack on Chemin des Dames in April, hampered by terrible weather. The miniscule gains for the loss of 130,000 dead and injured saw Nivelle sacked and replaced by Pétain, who had to rebuild shattered French morale and stave off the very real prospect of wholesale mutiny. It put the French out of any major offensive for the rest of the year.

The British fared better, making progress at Arras, most spectacularly with the Canadians' stunning capture of the vital high ground of

■ **ABOVE: The taking of Vimy Ridge, 1917. Canadian troops are seen advancing over no-man's land and through the German barbed wire whilst under fire.**

Vimy Ridge. But Haig failed to press home such a valuable gain and his forces experienced heavy casualties once again, including many Australians. The weary Allies could not afford to wait for the arrival of the American troops, however. By now enjoying greater freedom of operations separate from the French, the British began new offensives, first at Messines Ridge and then yet again at Ypres. The Messines attack in June, dependent on massive artillery barrages, was successful but only preliminary to the main assault in July, the Third Battle of Ypres, that came to be known as Passchendaele.

Even the melancholic sound of the name hints at the tragic loss of life. On a rain-sodden battlefield of cloying mud and putrid water, churned up by the 4.5 million shells fired by the Allies – not to mention those of the Germans – the sacrifice of life was numbing. By November, when the Canadians took the Passchendaele Ridge, the British and her imperial troops had lost nearly a quarter of a million men (the highest suffered by the British during the war), 70,000 of them dead. The Germans lost almost as many. Far from providing the decisive breakthrough to end the war,

such fighting only seemed to intensify its devastating cull of human life, and all for no real strategic gain.

Haig was undeterred however and sprang another assault at Cambrai on November 20, with the aim of unifying artillery, infantry and,

■ **ABOVE: Canadian machine gunners take over shell holes at Vimy Ridge, France, in April 1917.**

■ **BELOW: The Battle of Messines Ridge. British troops view the smashed remains of a German bunker and trenches, June 1917.**

for the first time, significant use of tanks. The assault was initially successful and church bells were even rung in Britain in celebration. But the delight was short-lived. The Germans would counterattack in 1918, regaining virtually all

the ground within two weeks.

Haig was pushed aside and Prime Minister Lloyd George, soon to be joined by French Premier Georges Clemenceau in the newly created Supreme War Council, was put in charge of overall war strategy, but the setbacks kept coming. The recently engaged ally Italy crumpled in the face of Austrian and then German attacks, with the defeat at Caporetto one of the most comprehensive in the whole war, and accompanied by massive losses. Only the introduction of valuable British and French divisions from the west saved Italy from complete collapse. By November, the Allies had lost Russia.

The news was better in the Middle East, but as 1917 drew to a close, it seemed the Americans could not arrive quickly enough.

■ **BELOW: A horse lies dead in the Flanders mud of Passchendaele, October 1917.**

Chapter Fourteen:

Here Come the Doughboys

January **1918** – November 9 **1918**

■ **ABOVE:** US Army General John J. Pershing, center, inspects French troops at Boulogne, France, June 13, 1917.

"Come on you sons of bitches! Do you want to live forever?"
– Dan Daly, 1ˢᵗ Sergeant, United States Marine Corps, June 4, 1918, in the fighting at Belleau Wood

The United States was a country where there had at first been widespread resistance to joining the European war. Millions of its immigrants – including those who traced German ancestry – had left Europe precisely to escape the kind of troubles and hardships that the "old countries" were plagued by. Yet, within months of declaring war, and after President Wilson's "14-points" peace plan had been sidelined in January 1918, America was probably the nation whose people were most committed to the fight, and to defeating the Germans once and for all.

America did not have a huge standing army – when it had declared war in 1917 it could muster a bare 100,000 men, while its industry was not geared toward war production. It would take time to recruit and equip a force of an initial 1 million men but, by June 1917, members of the American Expeditionary Force, the AEF, were arriving in France. Headed by General John J. Pershing, the numbers steadily grew at a rate of 300,000 a month. They were to prove decisive. They were nicknamed "doughboys" – the origin of the name is unclear but may relate to their well-fed and impressive physical state in contrast to the ailing and weary troops of the Allies. Healthy or not, thousands of American boys would soon suffer the same death their European counterparts had been incurring for nearly four years.

The situation in Europe was reaching its dramatic conclusion. With Russia out of the war, Germany could focus on the Western Front and draw on the industry and raw materials of the vast swathes of land it had won in the east. But social unrest back home was creating an altogether different phenomenon. Many German troops returning from the east had been inspired by the Russian Revolution and had similar plans for their own country. The submarine war, which German commanders believed would win them the overall war, had not gone to plan. Convoys of merchant ships protected by navy vessels had meant Britain didn't starve, while the more effective blockade of German ports was hitting the civilian population hard. Food queues in major cities illustrated the people's plight, while strikes and military mutinies started to break out.

Reflecting the growing sense of crisis was a split between the political arm of German authority, the Reichstag, and the military high command. Both sides sought some kind of peace but, while the Social Democratic party politicians desired a negotiated accord that would see Germany return to its pre-war borders, military leaders wanted to retain their conquests and create a "Greater Germany." In consequence the nationalist right-wing group, the Fatherland Party, was formed – an early example of the kind of movements that would plague Germany in the inter-war years and contribute to another conflict a generation later.

The head of the military government, Ludendorff, then played the "last card" in the hope of a victory that would secure those conquests in the east, and some of the territory captured from France. The German spring offensive was the first of three that year. Reinforced by divisions freed from action in the east, this bolstered German Army first targeted the southern flank of the British line near Amiens.

The tactics used were different to previous assaults however. A huge but relatively short bombardment of a small front honed in on command and communication centers as much as troops in the trenches. The resulting confusion would be followed by gas and smoke attacks, and assaults by shock troops or "storm troopers," armed with mortars, sled-carried guns, flamethrowers, and grenades. The regular infantry would then pour through and exploit the gap.

This embryonic form of blitzkrieg, or "lightning war" proved astonishingly successful, and the Germans drove 40 miles deep into French territory. For a while the

situation for the Allies appeared desperate, but Marshal Foch, who had effectively taken over as supreme Allied co-coordinator, stood firm and demanded resilience. With supply lines stretched, the German attack slowed and switched to the north, with the rapid recapture of the ground around Ypres that the Allies had sacrificed 400,000 men to take less than a year before.

Ludendorff's aim was to split the British and French armies and seize the Channel ports. The strategy appeared to be working as the British fell back and German heavy guns advanced to within range of Paris. But the Allied line – just – held. The offensive was switched to the French sector in what became the Third Battle of Aisne on May 27 but, while the Kaiser's troops made impressive gains, they had punched themselves to a virtual standstill. And, while they had made advances, there were the familiar massive losses – nearly half a million on both sides.

A key difference was that the Allies could reinforce. On May 28, the Americans joined the fight at Cantigny. It was a symbolic as well

■ **BELOW: British troops pass tanks in a French village close to Amiens following the German Kaiserschlacht offensive, 1918. Such was the vigor of their attack that they broke through the British line and pushed toward Amiens and the Channel ports. Amiens was only held following bitter fighting.**

as a strategic point in the war. With the French waging a flexible defense instead of the usual determination to hold every inch of ground, the Germans were forced back. Among their ranks, soldiers began to desert in droves. Now the momentum was firmly with the Allies. July saw a general offensive on all fronts by the Allies, and the Germans went into a fighting retreat. At Amiens, the British learned from the small-scale success at Le Hamel in July and married effective infantry and tank action, the use of low-flying aircraft, and improved artillery coordination to advance seven miles in one day. The dream of 1916 was at last realized. Ludendorff called it the "black day" for the German Army.

Losses were still crippling but the course of the war was set. On August 21, there was a breakthrough at Albert. In the south, in September, the Americans gained a stunning victory at St. Mihiel, albeit at high cost, before turning north. The Americans were brave, fit, and motivated, fighting with an enthusiasm not seen on the Western Front since 1914. Their

impact was decisive, helping to bleed the Germans dry. Germany had started the spring with 199 divisions but now had less than 50 capable of fighting on. Meanwhile, its ally, Austria-Hungary, was hurtling headlong into disarray and retreat in Italy, its army disintegrating in the field, hampered by desertions and with the people facing starvation in Vienna. With the front collapsing in Greece and the Balkans, Austria-Hungary sued for peace and signed itself out of the war on October 4. A day later the Allies captured the Hindenburg Line. Now Ludendorff pressed the Kaiser to negotiate an armistice – not surrender. The Allies were not in conciliatory mood, however, not least in America where there was a febrile clamor for victory once the lists of American dead began to grow.

In Berlin, matters came to a head. To head off the growing prospect of revolution, the Reichstag took full control, promising universal suffrage and with the Kaiser now reduced to a constitutional monarch. But it was too little too late. With army and government authority collapsing, the Kaiser was forced to abdicate on November 9. The end to the war was at last in sight.

■ BELOW: **American troops march through a town in the Meuse region of France, October 1918.**

Chapter Fifteen:
A Bitter Victory
November 11 **1918**

■ **ABOVE: The Allied representatives at the signing of the armistice. Ferdinand Foch, second from right, is seen outside his railway carriage in the forest of Compiègne, November 1918.**

With the Kaiser seeking exile in Holland, preparations were made for the final end to hostilities. On November 7, a delegation of German leaders and officers had traveled to Compiègne to discuss terms in a railway carriage. One of the party, Matthias Erzberger, would be assassinated by incensed German nationalists for his part in the affair. Before that, he and his colleagues were left in no doubt as to the Allies' intentions: agree to the surrender

terms or the war would be continued. Seventy-two hours later the relevant documents were signed. The announcement was made that firing would cease at 11am – the 11ᵗʰ hour, of the 11ᵗʰ day, of the 11ᵗʰ month.

"History has no more glorious day than yesterday, which saw the end of the Great World War and the triumph of Great Britain and her Allies," trumpeted the British newspaper the *Daily Mirror*. Yet, after four years of deafening, horrendous warfare, the

■ **ABOVE: United States Army soldiers, identified as troops of Company M, 6ᵗʰ Regular Infantry, celebrate in Remoiville, France, as the terms of the armistice are read, November 11, 1918.**

reaction was curiously mixed. Crowds celebrated in London, Paris, New York, and elsewhere, but there was not quite the universal joy that might have been expected on the front line. Soldiers sat around not quite knowing what to do. Prisoners of war came back to their own lines, some in strict parade drill style, others weakened by hunger barely able to move. The silence was eerie.

Servicemen on all sides were left to contemplate their extraordinary

> *"To me the most remarkable feature [was] the uncanny silence that prevailed. No rumbling of guns, no staccato of machine guns, nor did the roar of exploding dumps break into the night as it had so often done. The war was over."*
>
> **– Captain Llewellyn Evans, Royal Welsh Fusiliers**

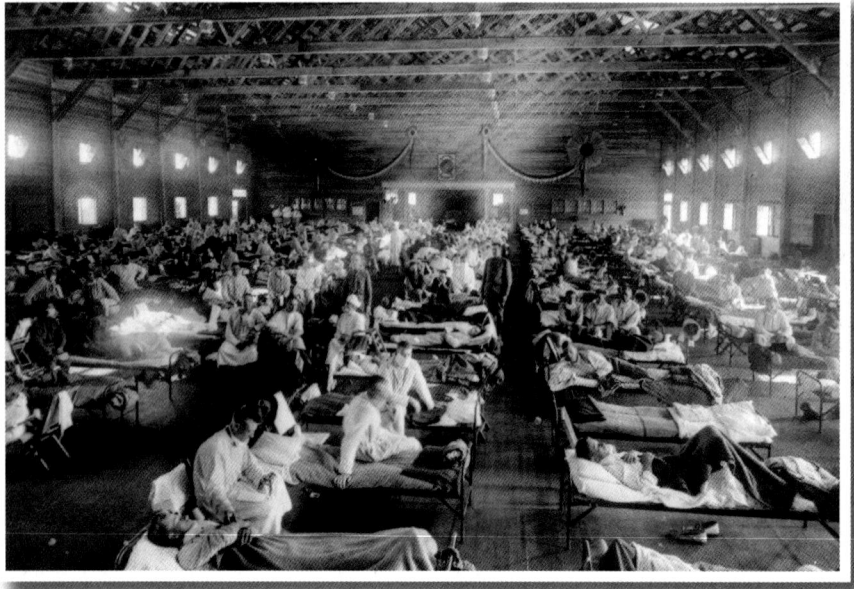

■ **ABOVE:** German submarines of the High Sea Fleet are seen here at Harwich, England, shortly after they surrendered, November 24, 1918.

■ **LEFT:** Influenza epidemic patients lie on cots at the emergency hospital in Camp Funston, Kansas, during the 1918 Spanish influenza outbreak.

experiences, their survival, and the loss of their friends. For so many had died. It is believed that the total death toll was 10 million, in addition to the near 9 million civilians who had been killed. The British lost around 750,000, together with 170,000 Australians, Canadians, New Zealanders, Indians, Africans, and other nationalities drawn from her empire. 1.8 million Germans were killed, along with 1.4 million French.

The Russians sacrificed 1.7 million, Italy 460,000, the USA 115,000 (in less than a year of fighting). Around 21 million were believed to have been hurt, many with appalling injuries: loss of limbs, blindness, and gas poisoning, not to mention the deep and long-lasting mental scars. In a cruel twist, millions more would die from a virulent influenza epidemic dubbed Spanish Flu that swept Europe and beyond in the immediate aftermath of war, taking another 8 million lives, many due to hunger and weakness caused by the war's privations.

There were many stories of tragedy and loss in World War I. The story of Second Lieutenant Walter Tull was just one among millions, but his sad demise seemed to sum up the heroism, desperate sadness, and crushing futility of the conflict. On March 25, 1918, amid the German advance on the old Somme battleground near Bapaume, Tull was one of 13 of the British 23rd Middlesex Battalion – the 2nd "Footballers Battalion" – who lost their lives. He had been shot through the head and though the men of his platoon, and in particular Private Billingham, a goalkeeper before the war, made courageous efforts to rescue Tull's body, the weight of the

■ BELOW: Walter Tull was one of Britain's first black soccer players. He was also the first black officer in the British Army, as well as the first black officer to lead white troops into battle in World War I. For his bravery, he was recommended the Military Cross and died a hero in the last Battle of the Somme in 1918, aged 29.

German advance forced them to leave his corpse behind.

Tull was a popular officer who inspired admiration and devotion from both officers and men. He first came to France in 1915 and had worked his way up thanks to his bravery and qualities of leadership. He suffered shell shock as a result of the First Battle of the Somme, but recovered to perform heroically in Italy before being sent back to the Western Front in 1918. One significance of his story was that Tull was a black man serving in the British Army and, as such, should not have been given a commission due to the color bar that existed at the time.

Commanding officers wanted to recommend Tull for the Military Cross but, thanks to a slight of hand, he did not qualify as, officially at least, he was not able to become an officer. There was not even a proper burial. Tull's body was one of the near 7 million that the mud had swallowed up or had simply disappeared across the various theaters, and for who there was no known last resting place.

There was another cruel irony in the Middle East, where one of the final defeats of the Turks came at a place synonymous with apocalyptic death and destruction. It was in September at Megiddo in Palestine – the place immortalized in the Bible that gave its name to the Greek word "Armageddon," signifying judgment day and the end of the world.

Whether in victory or defeat, for many it felt like their world had come to an end.

Chapter Sixteen:
Legacy
January 1919 – 1939

British Prime Minister David Lloyd George said, on Armistice Day, that he hoped the end of the Great War would signal the "end of all wars." He also wooed the voters with the promises to "build a land fit for heroes." In truth, neither was to be realized and, in many respects, the legacy of World War I was to sow the seeds for another, even ghastlier one 20 years later.

The victorious powers met in Paris in January 1919 for a series of conferences to create a peace that was troubled from the outset. There was an understandable desire in the west to see Germany punished and held in check, particularly in France, which had seen so much of its productive lands in the north devastated. The negotiators had to try and assemble a complicated geographical jigsaw, balancing competing interests and the wishes of peoples divided by language and ethnicity. The situation in the east was especially difficult, with the complex drawing of boundaries of a newly independent Poland, the isolation of German-speaking communities from the Fatherland, and the ongoing crisis posed by the Russian Revolution having direct consequences for future disputes.

There was terrible suffering in the Soviet Union, both in a brutal civil war (also known as the War of Allied Intervention), prosecuted by western governments to undermine the Bolsheviks, and the ruthless and totalitarian repressions that followed. The eventual settling of borders fed the tensions that led to World War II.

Attempts to broker a just peace were admirable but fraught with difficulty. The ideal of an international body committed to resolving disputes through negotiation was realized by the League of Nations set up by the

■ **ABOVE: The signing of the Peace Treaty. Shown here are British Prime Minister David Lloyd George and his French counterpart, Georges Clemenceau, at the Paris Peace Conference. Although discussions opened in December 1918, the Peace Conference did not formally open until January 18, 1919.**

Paris Peace Conference in 1919 but, while it had laudable aims, it was plagued by national interests from the start. The American senate rejected the League of Nations covenant, and a succession of nations would leave over the years.

Other people sought resolution through art and literature. The conflict produced some of the most outstanding war poetry from the likes of Wilfred Owen, Siegfried Sassoon, and A. E. Housman. Books and movies, such as *All Quiet On The Western Front*, gave moving voice to the experience of the common soldier. Canadian doctor John McCrae wrote one of the most memorable poems that came to embody the poignancy of the war.

But there was bitterness for many who survived to return home. The "Roaring Twenties" gave way to persistent economic problems and

■ **ABOVE:** **Signatories of the peace treaties at Paris (left to right): General Ferdinand Foch, Premier Georges Clemenceau, Prime Minister Lloyd George, Prime Minister Vittorio Orlando, and Sidney Sonnino, 1919.**

*"In Flanders field the poppies grow.
Between the crosses, row on row..."*
– Lieutenant Colonel John McCrae, **In Flanders Fields**

the Great Depression. Unsurprisingly, many servicemen felt betrayed and this in turn fed strikes, social strife, and political radicalism and extremism.

For the families who lost so many loved ones, the culture of remembrance grew. Ceremonies across the world would mark the day the guns fell silent, and memorials were struck in honor of those who had died. The vast cemeteries and monuments on the Western Front, such as the Menin Gate, the Thiepval Memorial, which honors 72,000 dead with no known graves, the St. Mihiel Military Cemetery, and Tyne Cot Cemetery, which is the resting place for 12,000 men, are all beautifully maintained and moving reminders of the war that are still visited by thousands today.

For other more elite families, the consequences of the war were terminal. The rule of the Tsars in Russia ended with assassination. The Habsburg clan that ruled Austria-Hungary saw their empire all but destroyed to be replaced with republics. The Ottoman Empire finally ended with the emergence of a new, secular Turkey. The British Royal Family, fearing anti-German sentiment, had already changed their dynastic name from Saxe-Coburg Gotha to the more Anglo-friendly Windsor. Their relation Kaiser Wilhelm, meanwhile, led a brooding life in exile for another 20 years in Holland.

He would witness, from a distance, the tumultuous changes taking place in his own country. The Treaty of Versailles, signed between the victors and the Allies on June 28, 1919, was regarded as too lenient by France and Britain, and too harsh by the Germans themselves. The American Senate refused to ratify it. The outcome was that the Rhineland was demilitarized and the Saar coalfields awarded to France. Germany was ordered to reduce her army to a rump of 100,000 men. The air force was abolished and her general staff disbanded, the navy rendered impotent. Lands that had been bitterly fought for were ceded, while the issue of "war guilt" caused furious resentment.

The war was estimated to have cost $260 billion and the Allies sought reparations of $63 billion, a figure finally agreed in 1921. The full bill was never paid, however. Instead, a new Germany was to emerge, many of its people crazed with a desire to atone for the loss of 1914–18 and fueled by dangerous conspiracy theories that put the blame on weak and traitorous democratic politicians supposedly controlled by "powerful Jews" around the world. It was the stuff of paranoid delusion, but it found ready adherents in a group of enraged ex-servicemen bent on vengeance.

Among them was a lance corporal who had been pictured among a crowd celebrating the start of the war in August 1914 in Munich. The photograph showed a 25-year-old smiling with joy at the prospect of war. His name was Adolf Hitler.

■ **RIGHT:** **The sun rises over wild poppies growing on the edge of a field at Thiepval in northern France, close to the Thiepval Memorial Monument.**

■ **ABOVE:** **Adolf Hitler, among the crowd in the Odeonsplatz, Munich, when war was declared, August 2, 1914.**

Sources

1915 by Lyn Macdonald (Headline, 1993)
Echoes of War by Robert Giddings (Bloomsbury, 1992)
Somme by Lyn Macdonald (Papermac, 1984)
The First World War by Michael Howard (OUP, 2002)
The First World War by David Evans (Hodder Education, 2004)
Trench by Stephen Bull (Osprey, 2010)
Walter Tull, Officer, Footballer by Phil Vasili (Raw Press, 2010)

BBC
spartacus.schoolnet.co.uk
Dictionary of 20th Century History (OUP, 1992)
Dictionary of 20th Century World Biography (OUP, 1992)

Introduction

When World War I began, many people thought it would be over within months. Some among the millions of eager young men who flocked to recruitment offices across Europe even feared they would miss out on the action when the great powers lined up for conflict. Four long, terrible years later, many of those idealistic but doomed souls would not survive to tell the tale of what they did experience in the Great War.

A century after the guns fell silent, relive and discover the drama, devastation, and tragedy of the war to end all wars. Witness the conflict's fighting in its various theaters, its impact on the home front, and some of its heroes, villains, and those ordinary people in extraordinary times.

47

Men who fell covering the retreat of the 5th Army at Albert during the Hun offensive in 1918.

The Somme, 1918 – and yet more soldiers are added to the roll call of the dead.

The March to War

Verkündung des Kriegszustandes
durch Leutnant von Viebahn in Berlin, Unter den Linden
2632

The clamor for war reached a fever pitch as the big European nations limbered up for a climactic showdown that had been years in the making. In Germany, a young country bursting with patriotic fervor and with rulers greedy for conquest, millions flocked to the cause. On Berlin's Unter den Linden in August 1914, crowds greeted the tumultuous news that they were now at war with England, France, and Russia.

One of the inevitable features of the war was the propaganda on both sides that demonized the enemy. British mockery of the Germans was initially rather innocuous, portraying the average German male as either very plump, very thin, over militaristic, or simply just unfit for fighting, hence the phrase "Gott help us!" This comparatively modest ridicule soon gave way to more impassioned and strident outrage, responding to the widely believed stories and rumors that the Kaiser's troops were savagely brutal.

The pressure to sign up and join the fight was evident from the start of the war. Recruitment campaigns – as on this cigarette card – exploited the guilt young men would face if they were not seen to be "doing their bit" in failing to defend their country's cause.

The Opening Shots

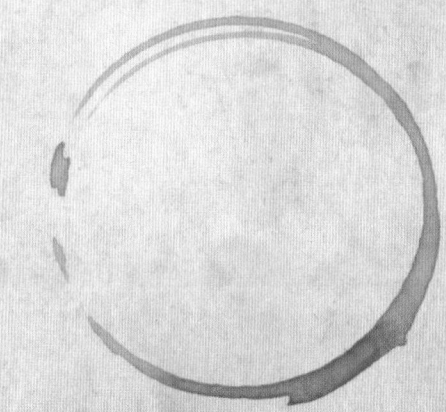

Through the millennia, soldiers have looked for omens and have placed their faith in the supernatural, and World War I was no exception. One of the most famous stories arose in August 1914, when, during the inspirational fighting retreat of the BEF around Mons, a legend emerged of the ghostly appearance of angels protecting the British. Brigadier General Charteris claimed, " the angel of the Lord on the traditional white horse, and clad all in white with flaming sword, faced the advancing Germans at Mons and forbade their further progress."

The civilian cost soon became apparent. The German invasion through Belgium caused immense suffering for non-combatants, who fled for their lives into Antwerp. Just days after this photograph was taken, however, the major Channel port fell to the invaders.

Wishful thinking on the part of one propagandist, imagining the Kaiser being squeezed on all fronts in a vice-like Allied grip.

"To Arms!"

'YOU ARE THE MAN I WANT'

As the initial pace of volunteering for the British armed forces slowed, Lord (later to become Earl in 1914) Kitchener was the public face demanding a boost in recruitment. As minister of war, Kitchener warned the war would last years and pushed for a massive increase in troop numbers. With opponents in the government, he was removed from the command of military strategy in 1915.

All manner of methods were used to encourage, compel, and virtually shame men into joining up. Londoners were even threatened with the rejection of their sweethearts, who were manipulated into thinking their boyfriend was spurning them if he wasn't "wearing khaki."

TO THE YOUNG WOMEN OF LONDON

Is your "Best Boy" wearing Khaki? If not don't **YOU THINK** he should be?

If he does not think that you and your country are worth fighting for—do you think he is **WORTHY** of you?

Don't pity the girl who is alone—her young man is probably a soldier—fighting for her and her country—and for **YOU.**

If your young man neglects his duty to his King and Country, the time may come when he will **NEGLECT YOU.**

Think it over—then ask him to

JOIN THE ARMY TO-DAY

Printed by David Allen & Sons Ltd., Harrow, London, etc.

Such tactics worked and the ranks of the British Army were swelled, as seen in this chaotic scene from Southwark Town Hall in London. Numbers were maintained by the introduction of the draft or "conscription." Many signed up with their workmates or friends from the same area. Lord Derby promoted such a scheme, beginning in 1916, which led to the formation of the famous "Pals Battalions."

On the Eastern Front, deeply religious Russian soldiers kissed icons before going into battle. The war in the east was a ferocious slaughter, with the Russians incurring huge casualties in a series of epic battles.

Commanders and Leaders

MARSHAL FOCH
From a photograph by Demay

Eyeing up the prospects for the Germans through a periscope was Field Marshal Paul von Hindenburg. Raised among Prussian aristocratic circles, von Hindenburg oversaw spectacular victories on the Eastern Front, in conjunction with his outstanding tactician Major-General Erich von Ludendorff (pictured alongside him), before the pair were switched to command in the west.

"l' offensive a l'outrance" - "attack at all costs" - was the mantra of French commander General Ferdinand Foch. The tactic led to devastating losses at the start of the war but, as the conflict reached its crescendo in 1918, he was appointed commander of Allied forces and was in the post when victory was gained.

Le Petit Journal

ADMINISTRATION
61, RUE LAFAYETTE, 61
Les manuscrits ne sont pas rendus
On s'abonne sans frais
dans tous les bureaux de poste

15 CENT.
29me Année

SUPPLÉMENT ILLUSTRÉ

15 CENT.
Numéro 1445

ABONNEMENTS
France et Colonies.... 5 fr. 6 fr.
Étranger .... 8 fr. 10 fr.

DIMANCHE 1er SEPTEMBRE 1918

LES CHEFS VICTORIEUX

LE MARÉCHAL DOUGLAS HAIG

Le Général DEBENEY
(1re Armée française)

Le Général H. RAWLINSON
(4e Armée anglaise)

Le Général HUMBERT
(3e Armée française)

French publication Le Petit Journal celebrated a number of Allied commanders including General Marie Debeney of the 1st French Army, General Sir Henry Rawlinson, and General Georges Humbert of the 3rd French Army. The main picture is of General Douglas Haig, for many critics the man synonymous with the human waste of the conflict for his decision to commit huge numbers of troops to repeated, yet largely fruitless, attacks.

1915

The global nature of the war meant troops from a number of colonized nations were either brought into combat to serve their imperial rulers, or to fight at home - as with these Cameroonian troops fighting with the British in West Africa in 1915.

The British sought to open up a new front in the Mediterranean by attacking Turkey through the Dardanelles at Gallipoli. The original caption for this photograph was "short of ammunition but still they press on, the true bulldog rush of our troops," but behind the naive patriotism was a bitter truth: the campaign was a disaster for the Allies.

New weapons made their presence on the battlefield. This Clement Talbot armored car was a forerunner of a machine that would go on to have a far greater impact on modern warfare.

The war of attrition on the Western Front devastated whole swathes of Flanders and France. Sermaize les Bains on the ravaged Marne had been virtually obliterated by 1915.

1914-15... SERMAIZES-LES-BAINS | 1914-15... SERMAIZES-LES-BAINS

36me Série

Aces High!

World War I produced a new theater of conflict in the skies. As courageous men fought astonishing battles in the air, there soon emerged a new breed of war hero – the flying ace. Foremost among them all was Manfred von Richthofen, the legendary "Red Baron." He was credited with a remarkable 80 "kills" before he himself was shot down and killed in April 1918.

Lieutenant William Leefe-Robinson was the dashing British airman who was awarded the Victoria Cross for shooting down a German Zeppelin over the fields of Hertfordshire, just to the north of London. He survived combat but was one of the millions of victims of the influenza pandemic that swept the world, soon after the war's end.

Destroyer of a Zeppelin near London.

THE HERO OF THE HOUR IN ENGLAND : LIEUT. WILLIAM LEEFE ROBINSON, V.C.

Like Lieut. Warneford, who won the V.C. for destroying a Zeppelin near Ghent, Lieut. Robinson, V.C., was born in India. He is just twenty-one, and was at Sandhurst when the war broke out, getting his commission in the Worcesters in December 1914. Taking up aviation, he joined the Royal Flying Corps, and saw active service in France as an observer during the summer of last year. He obtained his pilot's certificate just a year ago this month, in September 1915, and was appointed a Flying Officer in the R.F.C. For several months past he has been attached to various stations for night flying. He is one of the most unaffected and modest of men, and does not know what fuss means in the discharging of his duties.—[Photo. by L.N.A.]

France's greatest air ace was George Guynemer, who flew over 600 missions and was shot down six times. He is seen here in 1917, in his Nieuport aircraft.

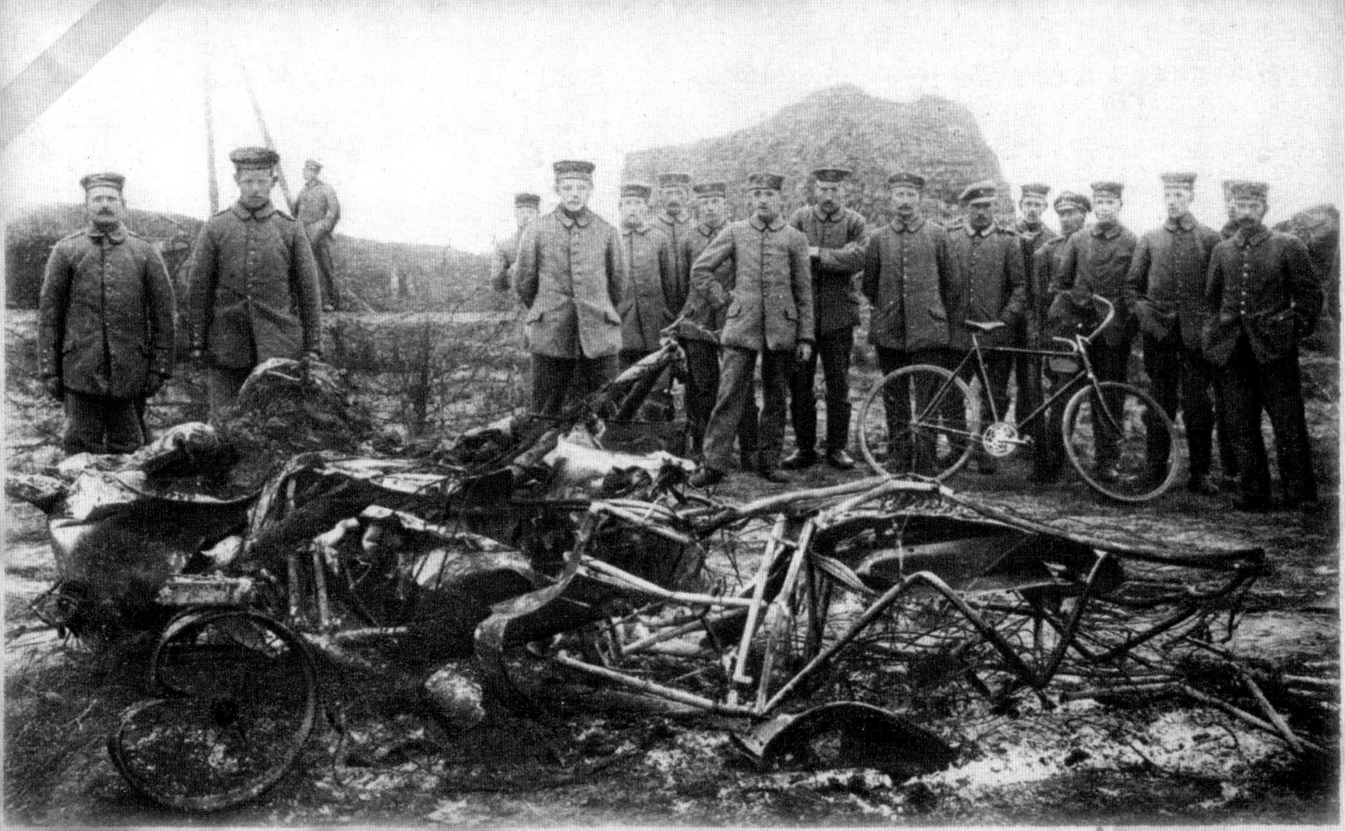

Air aces captured the imagination of the public but all too often paid the ultimate sacrifice: the wreckage of the plane flown by German fighter pilot Max Immelmann – dubbed "the Eagle of Lille" – in June 1916.

88 GUERRE DE 1914. — Aero-mitrailleuse Deperdussin
LL.
Reproduction interdite

This machine gunner in a French Deperdussin monoplane was exposed to the elements as well as to the enemy.

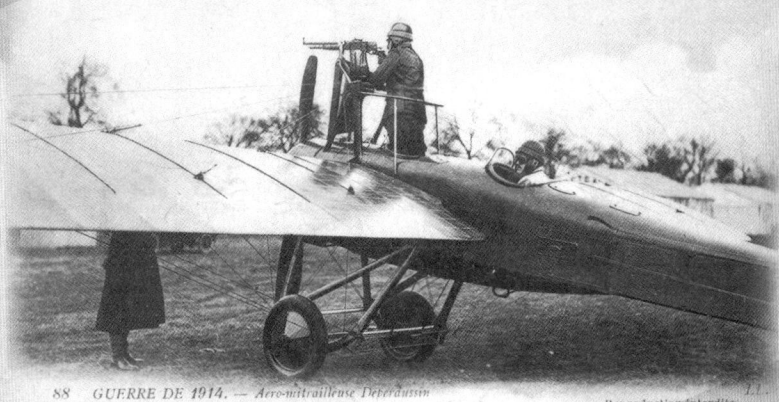

Gas!

Away from the idealized romance of the air war, life – and death – on the ground took a sickening twist with the advent of chemical warfare, in the form of gas attacks. Early masks provided some but not enough protection, while giving the wearer a horrific and frightening appearance.

The Germans first used gas against the Russians and introduced it onto the Western Front in 1915. The tactic soon spread so that an escalation in the development and use of gas created a terrifying new dimension to life in the trenches.

A GERMAN GAS-ATTACK PHOTOGRAPHED BY AN AIRMAN : POISONOUS FUMES ROLLING TOWARDS THE RUSSIANS ; AND GERMAN TROOPS.

This very remarkable photograph was taken by a Russian airman in flight, and shows the beginning of a gas-attack made by the Germans. The poisonous clouds are seen as they are rolling towards the Russian lines after having been liberated from cylinders worked by the men seen behind the fumes. Behind these men are three lines of the enemy, waiting to attack after the gas has done its work. No better proof can be wanted of the statements that the enemy are using gas not only on the Western front, but on the Eastern. In a case like this, gas is liberated from specially contrived cylinders, when the wind is blowing towards the desired position. It is always possible that a sudden change of wind may cause the enemy to be hoist by their own petard.—[Photo. supplied by C.N.]

A remarkable aerial shot showing the deadly progression of a gas cloud released against Russian forces.

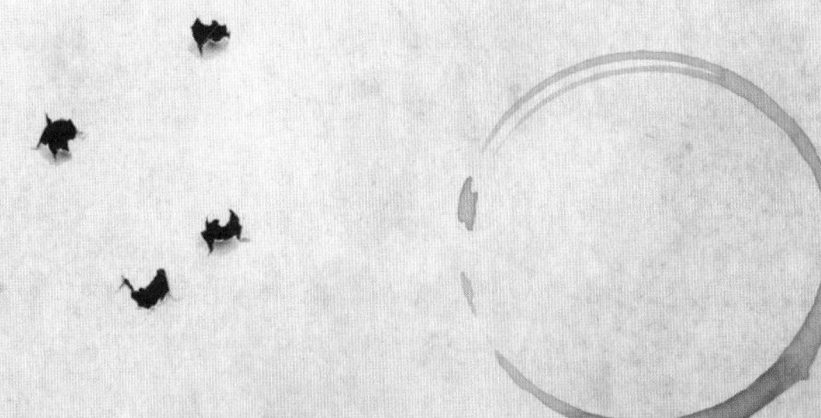

1916

Our gallant infantry charging the German positions.

1916 would prove to be another ghastly year. In a concerted attempt to break the stalemate of trench warfare, the British opened up a massive offensive on the Somme in the summer, but with disastrous consequences. On the first day alone, there were 57,000 casualties – the worst in the whole history of the British Army, and for miniscule, futile gains. The carnage created a surreal and lifeless landscape. Soldiers carried spades to make fresh trenches that had to be dug after every attack.

British infantrymen lie dead in this graphic image of the immediate aftermath of an attack on a German position.

"No-Man's Land."

The Somme campaign ended with both sides still waging a daily struggle to survive in the trenches. This portrait of "the Trench Train" may have been idealized, but it movingly illustrated the sorrow of soldiers having to leave their loved ones at London's Victoria Station, before they headed back to the nightmare existence on the front line.

FRANK DALD

Trenches

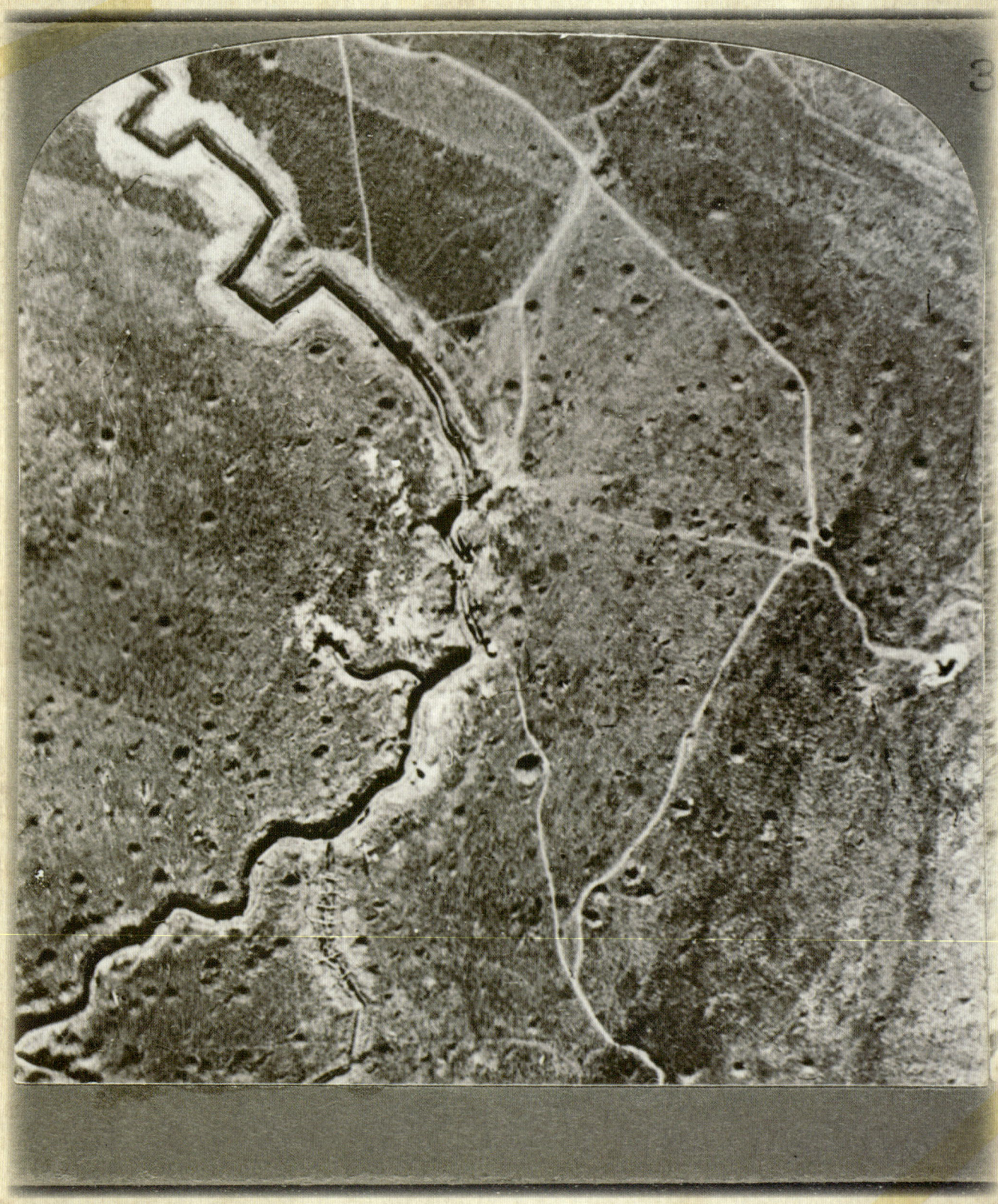

Seen from the air, the lines of German trenches wriggle across the Western Front, amid a shell-pitted and bomb-cratered terrain.

FIGHTING THE RAIN AND THE FLOODS: BALING IN THE BRITISH TRENCHES.

Rain and snow and slush do not tend to comfort in the trenches, though the troops make the best of it and everything possible is done to mitigate the conditions. Recently, it is said, wader-stockings have been ordered, and various means are taken to keep the trenches reasonably dry. "The problem of how best to get rid of the water," wrote "Eye-Witness" recently, "is one which is engaging the

LIKE A GIGANTIC SOUP-LADLE: A BRITISH IMPLEMENT FOR BALING IN THE TRENCHES.

attention of both sides. Muddy water has been found difficult to pump, but this difficulty is being overcome. Continual baling and pumping are required." Again, he says: "As a consequence of the recent heavy and almost continuous rain, the struggle against the forces of Nature has assumed almost greater importance than that being waged against the enemy."—[Photos. by Newspaper Illustrations.]

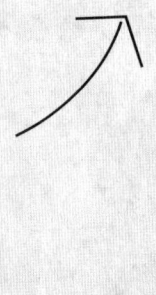

Divided by conflict, united in suffering. German (left) and British troops faced a never-ending struggle to try and stop the trenches from becoming flooded and fetid quagmires in wet weather.

Both sides faced terrible privations trying to eke out an existence in the trenches. Shattered dugouts could become tombs if hit by the remorseless artillery fire while, for those who survived, their lives were pitiful.

The shared misery and the genuine desire to fight for their brothers-in-arms meant that soldiers formed incredibly strong bonds of friendship in the trenches. Enjoying the blessed relief of a smoke, somewhere in Flanders during a brief period of rest away from the front line, is a group of British "Tommies," listening to a tune on the accordion. Popular songs of the time included, Pack Up Your Troubles In Your Old Kit Bag and It's A Long Way To Tipperary.

Trenches were plagued by vermin - "a greater trench-worry than the Germans were the rats," according to the original caption to this photo. These French soldiers showed off their kills in a graphic illustration of the battle against the deadly pests.

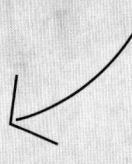

The redoubtable British Tommy in the trenches.

War at Sea

Despite – or perhaps because of – the enormous size of the great navies of the era, major battles at sea were relatively rare. Britain's determination to maintain her mastery of the oceans kept the powerful German fleet in check and largely in harbor, but the Royal Navy did not have the freedom to decide the conflict in the way it had done in centuries past.

One major confrontation that did take place was at Jutland; one of the heroic stories to emerge from this indecisive battle concerned the exploits of 16-year-old Jack Cornwell, who bravely stood at his post on HMS Chester despite being mortally wounded. He posthumously received the Victoria Cross for his valor.

U-boats were a deadly menace against Allied shipping. U-8 was held responsible for sinking HMS Pathfinder during the early months of the war.

Destruction of German U-boats was prized. This submarine was driven inshore and blown out of the water in 1917.

The Lusitania at sea. A British luxury liner, she was sunk off the coast of Ireland without warning by a German submarine in 1915, leading to great loss of life including that of 128 Americans. The attack pushed the USA closer toward conflict with the Central Powers. The vessel was sunk as a consequence of the Germans' decision to mount all-out submarine warfare against Allied shipping, a tactic later resumed in 1917, which further compelled the Americans to join the conflict.

1917

In 1917, the Germans pulled back from the Western Front to construct a new defensive position called the "Siegfried" or "Hindenburg" Line. Rather than the familiar unbroken stretch of thin trenches, it was formed of heavily fortified machine gun and artillery points, including concrete pillboxes, such as this one at Bullecourt. It was the scene of heavy fighting during the Battle of Arras.

The vivid drama of going "over the top," a familiar and terrifying experience for troops, this time at Wytschaete Wood in Belgium, during the Messines offensive.

Zero hour! Prompt to the second, our men go over the top in a grand assault on Wytschaete Wood.

Guarding sacred Ypres, where British heroism shone resplendent through war's darkest hours.

Ypres, or "Wipers" as it was dubbed by the British foot soldiers, was the scene of numerous bloody battles through the war. By 1917, it had been left a battered and highly evocative shell.

Home Front

Between 1914-18, war involved civilian populations to a greater extent than it had in previous conflicts – with non-combatants a frequent target. Even places far away from the front line could come under fire, as with this row of houses in Hartlepool, northeast England, which were shelled by German naval guns in December 1914.

GERMANY'S BOMBARDMENT OF PRIVATE HOUSES AND SLAUGHTER OF CIVILIANS : A HOUSE IN CLEVELAND ROAD, HARTLEPOOL, WRECKED BY SHELLS.

At the inquests on the victims of the German bombardment of Hartlepool, the evidence showed that they were killed, some in their homes or workshops, and others in the streets. The residential parts of Hartlepool suffered most. Few public buildings were hit, the streets of shops were hardly touched, and the docks and yards also escaped with little damage. What should have been the chief target of the German guns, and the only pretext for bombarding Hartlepool—that is, the battery guarding the harbour entrance—was not struck at all. The German exploit consisted chiefly in slaughtering a large number of unarmed civilians, including women and children. Our photograph shows an example of the havoc caused by the German shells in the homes of non-combatants.—[Photo. by Newspaper Illustrations.]

Children at home were often portrayed in poignant scenes deliberately designed to touch a chord with families. This father and daughter were dubbed "two gallant Tommies."

"CHUMS"

Two gallant Tommies here you see
For dangers neither cares a rap.
We'll meet the foe, where'er he be,
With soldier heart and soldier cap.

World War I was a war fought on an industrial scale. Across the globe, factories were committed to the war effort and, with men away fighting, women often formed the mainstay of the workforce. Here, a group of women pause for the camera at a British munitions factory.

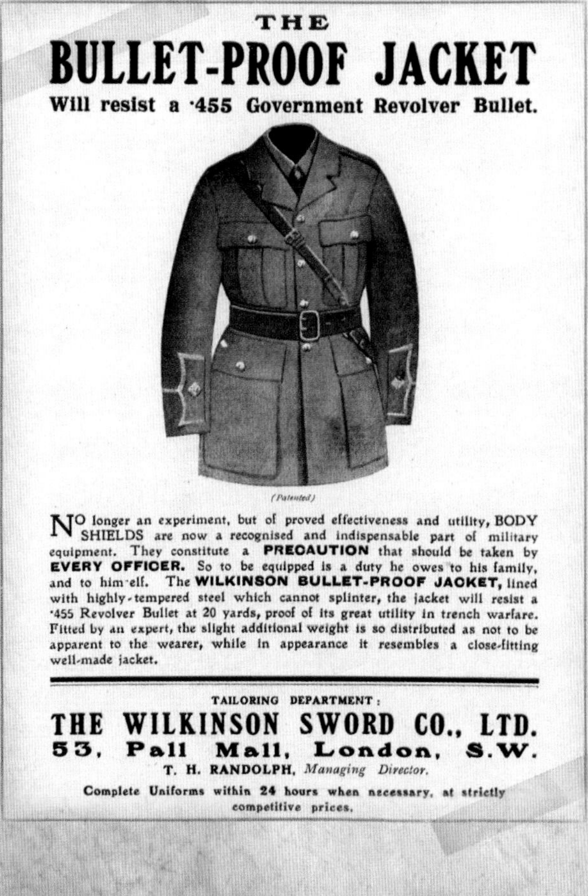

THE
BULLET-PROOF JACKET
Will resist a ·455 Government Revolver Bullet.

(Patented)

NO longer an experiment, but of proved effectiveness and utility, BODY SHIELDS are now a recognised and indispensable part of military equipment. They constitute a PRECAUTION that should be taken by EVERY OFFICER. So to be equipped is a duty he owes to his family, and to himself. The WILKINSON BULLET-PROOF JACKET, lined with highly-tempered steel which cannot splinter, the jacket will resist a ·455 Revolver Bullet at 20 yards, proof of its great utility in trench warfare. Fitted by an expert, the slight additional weight is so distributed as not to be apparent to the wearer, while in appearance it resembles a close-fitting well-made jacket.

TAILORING DEPARTMENT:
THE WILKINSON SWORD CO., LTD.
53, Pall Mall, London, S.W.
T. H. RANDOLPH, Managing Director.

Complete Uniforms within 24 hours when necessary, at strictly competitive prices.

An advert for a "bullet-proof jacket." It promised to be able to "resist a 455 government revolver bullet. No longer an experiment, but of proved effectiveness and utility, BODY SHIELDS are now a recognised and indispensable part of military equipment. They constitute a PRECAUTION that should be taken by EVERY OFFICER. So to be equipped is a duty he owes to his family, and to himself. The Wilkinson bullet-proof jacket, lined with highly-tempered steel which cannot splinter. Available from Wilkinson Sword, Pall Mall, London."

1918

Here come the Yanks:
A US Navy recruitment poster signaled the arrival of American forces that would play a major part in turning the outcome of the war.

British artillery being moved into position in 1918. By now, shelling techniques had been improved with greater accuracy, timing, and focus.

The weight of Allied armies eventually told and Germany was forced to admit defeat. On November 11, 1918, Marshal Foch headed a group of delegates in the forests of Compiègne, to sign the terms of the surrender.

A graphic representation of the cost of victory.

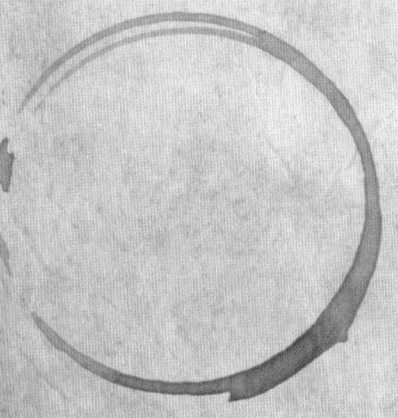

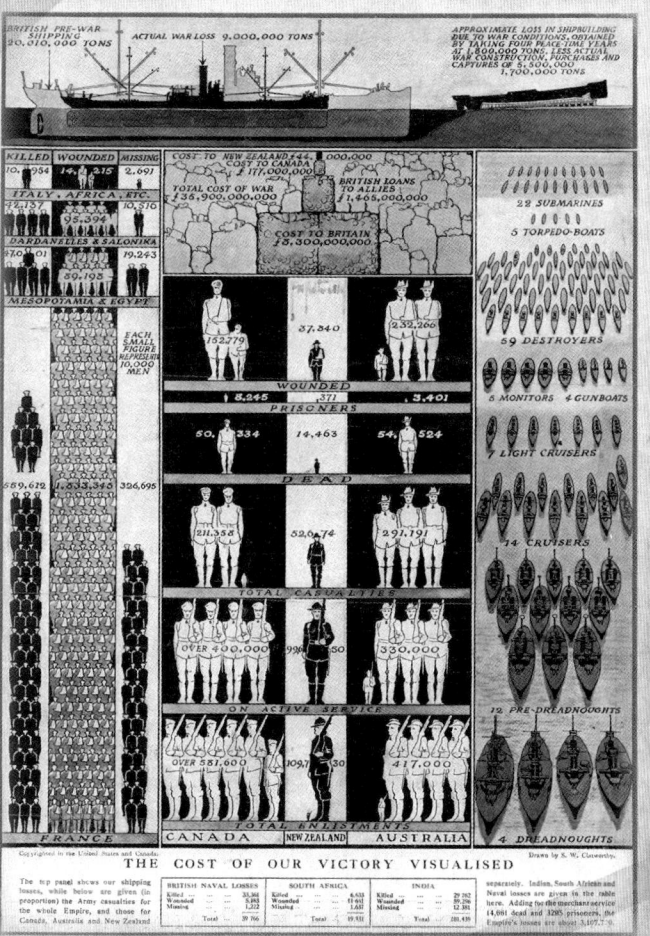

THE COST OF OUR VICTORY VISUALISED

Aftermath

Thousands thronged the streets of London for the Peace Parade of 1918.

One of the true costs of war: a group of soldiers blinded by gas attacks. They were pictured at St. Dunstan's hostel, in Regent's Park, London. St. Dunstan's was set up by Mr. C. Arthur Pearson, in order to rehabilitate blinded soldiers, to help them acquire the skills for everyday life, and to help them learn a trade in order to eventually find employment in a more peaceful world.

In Flanders Fields... The poignant scene of a field full of poppies after World War I.